Look, No Hans

C000300770

A Comedy

John Chapman

and

Michael Pertwee

Samuel French - London
New York - Toronto - Hollywood

LOOK, NO HANS!

First presented at the Yvonne Arnaud Theatre, Guildford, by arrangment with Michael Codron. Subsequently presented by Michael Codron at the Strand Theatre, London, on 4th September, 1985, with the following cast of characters:

Fisher	David Jason
Kurt*	Tom Eastwood
Heidi	Heather Alexander
Monica	Lynda Bellingham
Cadwallader	Richard Vernon
Mitzi	Anita Graham
Tregunter-Jones	Charmian May
Foot†	Michael Shilling

Directed by Mike Ockrent
Designed by Poppy Mitchell

The action of the play takes place in a combined living-room and office in a large apartment in West Berlin

ACT I   A hot morning in August
ACT II Immediately following

Time—the present

*The part of Kurt is voice only
†The part of Foot is optional (only his legs need be seen)

COPYRIGHT INFORMATION

(See also page ii)

ACT I

A combined living-room and office in a large apartment in West Berlin. A hot August morning

It is a large, spacious apartment of pre-war German architecture. All the doors are of solid mahogany. About three feet below the back wall is a large wooden-framed archway almost the width of the room. Through the arch, in the centre of the back wall, is the front door, which has a letter box and a bell. There is an exit off to L of the front door, which leads to bedrooms and bathrooms. To one side of the front door is a hat-stand with the odd hat and coat on it. The entire hall behind the archway is on a raised dais

In the L wall of the room are two doors. One UL leads to a large walk-in cupboard. Below that is another door which leads to the kitchen. The cupboard opens onstage, the kitchen door offstage. Below the kitchen door is the drinks table. In the angle of R wall and back wall there is an impressive, high window with french windows opening on to a balcony outside. DR an archway leads to a bedroom

On stage R is a knee-hole desk and chair with telephone and an intercom with loudspeaker. Centre stage is a sofa. There are one or two other chairs and occasional tables and a filing cabinet. A connection with the motor business is indicated by a poster which shows a brand new model of a car under bold printing: MIDLAND MOTORS—NEW CYCLONE. *Behind the desk on the wall is a large coloured poster of the Matterhorn*

When the Curtain rises, the stage is empty and the radio is playing "The Ride of the Valkyries". The french windows and front door are open, the other doors are closed

Peter Fisher enters carrying a handful of assorted letters; he is sifting through them. Fisher is a pleasant fellow, perhaps not too bright, but willing and cheerful despite the fact that he is trying to sell British cars to the Germans. The top drawer of the filing cabinet is open. He pops some papers and letters into it and shuts it. As he walks away to turn the radio off, the second drawer slowly opens. He doesn't notice it. He turns the radio off

The intercom speaker bursts into life with Kurt's Voice. Kurt is only a voice throughout the play and has a strong German accent

Kurt's Voice Kurt from showroom calling Herr Fisher. Kurt from showroom calling Herr Fisher.

Fisher goes to the desk and flips the switch

Fisher Yes Kurt?

Kurt's Voice Ah, guten morgen, Herr Fisher. Happy birthday. Der showroom is empty.

Fisher Any other cheering items of news?

Kurt's Voice Nein, but it has gone ten . . .

Fisher (*copying the German accent*) And you want your elevenses.

Kurt's Voice Ja. I am going to the Weinstube.

Fisher OK, and when you come back like a lion refreshed, you can do me a favour.

Kurt's Voice Anything.

Fisher I am well aware that trying to sell British cars in Germany is like selling pork chops at a barmitzvah, but it doesn't help to have the showroom window so filthy that people can't even see what they're not going to buy.

Kurt's Voice You are making a very good point there.

Fisher Glad you agree—so wash it!

Kurt's Voice Herr Fisher, I am a salesman, not a window cleaner.

Fisher You've been promoted.

Kurt's Voice (*without realizing*) Oh, thank you!

Fisher Don't mention it. (*He flips the "Off" switch, then sifts through the letters*) Bills . . . bills . . . bills. (*Then, with a chuckle*) Oh well, they're not mine. They're Bill's. (*He drops them into a waste-paper basket, sits at the desk and suddenly notices an envelope half hidden under some papers*) What's this? (*A quick glance at it causes him to react nervously. He rips open the letter and looks at it*) It's the damn code! Codebook . . . codebook . . . (*He hurries to the filing cabinet, sifting through the keys in his pocket. He eventually finds the right one, turns to insert it into the second drawer and is surprised to see it is open*) Oh, that's handy. (*He takes out a codebook, returns to the desk, sits down and starts decoding the letter*) Four—five—seven—three. (*He checks with the codebook*) "Dear". Seven—eight—one—two—eight—seven—seven. (*He checks the codebook*) "Flasher". (*He reacts and checks again*) Oh, "Fisher". Three—two—three—five—one—zero. (*He checks the codebook*) "Operation imminent". (*He reads again*) "Dear Fisher, Operation imminent . . ."

There is a ring at the front doorbell. Hastily, Fisher puts the letter and paper into the book and runs to the filing cabinet, where he puts the book into the 2nd drawer. He begins to close drawer 2—it sticks. Drawer 1 opens (both drawers are open together). Fisher tries to close both drawers. Momentarily they stick, then close. He opens the front door

> *Outside stands Heidi, a glamorous German girl with an attractive accent. She is casually but expensively dressed, and carries a handbag and a small parcel*

Heidi Peter, darling! Happy birthday!

Heidi kisses him, presents him with the small parcel, then immediately hurries DS *to the sofa*

Come here, my liebchen, and I will give you another present.

She removes her jacket, kicks off her shoes, with the evident intention of getting down to a romantic session straight away. Having closed the door, Fisher sees what she is up to and reacts in dismay

Fisher Heidi! Are you crazy? Everything's off. Put everything on. My wife may walk in.

Heidi (*startled*) You said she was going to England!

Fisher She was—is—but the plane's been delayed a couple of hours. She's just out shopping. (*He undoes the present*) Oh, hankies, how lovely, just what I always wanted.

Heidi In that case I am going up on the roof to sunbathe. Join me as soon as you can.

Fisher But your husband ...

Heidi Otto will not be back until twelve. That gives us two hours; enough to make love four times!

Fisher Give or take three ... Listen, Heidi, didn't you get my flowers?

Heidi Oh yes, such a beautiful big bunch of orchids, but I threw them out of the window into the canal. (*She indicates out of the window, below which we assume is the canal*)

Fisher I can't say I blame you, but I just felt I had to send you some little memento.

Heidi If Otto comes back and sees orchids he would go mad. He would kill anyone who looked at me.

Fisher Kill? I don't want to carp, but I wish you'd mentioned that before.

Heidi It is so sad I had to throw your flowers away, but at least I have kept your little card, and it made me so happy.

Fisher (*staggered*) It did? It shouldn't have.

Heidi It means you are going to leave your wife and we shall run away together, no?

Fisher (*almost a shriek*) No! How ... (*He controls himself*) How could you read that into it?

Heidi I remember every word. I have kept the card here, next to my heart. (*She delves for the card in the top of her dress*)

Fisher Could I have a peep? I forget the exact words.

Heidi takes a white card from her cleavage. She reads from it

Heidi (*reading*) "I am counting the hours until we are together again. Life without you is no life at all. All my love, Peter."

Fisher (*snatching the card from her*) The idiots! They mixed the cards!

Heidi Mixed them? (*Furiously*) You are sending flowers also to another voman?

Fisher No! Yes! Not to a *voman*—to my vife.

Heidi You gave her also orchids?

Fisher No! No! A simple little posy.

Heidi Then what did my card say?

Fisher (*awkwardly*) The fact is ... I felt we might be getting too fond of each other ... that we should break if off before someone got hurt ... after all, I do love Monica, and you love Otto ...

Heidi I hate him!

Fisher Oh. Well, perhaps he may grow on you.

Heidi (*eyes brimming*) You think I would have given all of myself to you if I had still loved Otto? (*She hangs her handbag on Fisher's arm and uses one of the handkerchiefs bought for him to blow her nose*)

Fisher Well, at the time I didn't give it much thought.

Heidi I can see now. You have just been toying with me.

They both blow their noses noisily

Fisher Let's be fair, Heidi, I only toyed once.

Heidi Let's make it twice.

Fisher All right. But only once. And later! Now please go, Heidi. (*He starts to push her to the front door*) I've got to call that damned flower shop. If Monica reads what I wrote on your card, she'll hit the roof.

Heidi All right; but remember, I am *on* the roof. As soon as I see her leave, I shall come down for you.

Fisher Yes, yes.

Fisher pushes Heidi out of the front door and closes it. He notices her bag on his arm, opens the door and gives it back to her

Heidi Danke.

Heidi exits

Fisher Danke. (*He shuts the door*) Why do we do these things? (*He sits at the desk and dials a number, reading from the card*) Sieben, sieben, zwei, zwei, acht! What a messy language. (*He wipes the desk. While waiting he pours himself a large whisky from a bottle concealed in a drawer of the desk. He takes a gulp, neat. On the phone*) Hello? Ja. Could I speak to the Fraulein who speaks English, please? . . . She's aus? . . . Oh, damn! Well, here goes. Allo! Ich bin Herr Fisher, und early this morgen I telefunked du fur zwei bunchen of blumen fur zwei different damen—ein grosse und ein kleine . . . No! Not grosse dame! Eine grosse und ein kleine bunchen of *blumen* . . . Ja. Und du hast ge-cockened it up. . . . Well fur ein start der kleine bunchen hasn't even been ge-livered yet, und when it dost there will be ein grosse bangen. . . . Why? Because du hast attached der second carten to der firsta grosse bunchen; so the wrong dama got it . . . Get it? Good. Zo, der pointen ist, has du jetzt sent der firsta carten mit der kleine bunchen of blumen to the other dama, or is there still time to stop it? . . . Du hast? (*He visibly slumps*) Und der isn't? . . . Danke. You have just dropped me in the blumen ge-fertiliser. (*He slams down the phone*)

Simultaneously, the front door opens to reveal Monica Fisher, who enters with a shopping basket. Monica is the well brought up daughter of a vicar; naïve at times, over-effusive at times, and a thorough-going "good sort"

Ge-God! Ge-Monica! Good-morning! Why am I saying good-morning? We said that already.

Monica Are you all right? What's that you're drinking?

Fisher It said whisky on the label.

Monica At ten-thirty in the morning?
Fisher It says it all the time. You look radiant. (*He looks at his watch*)
Shouldn't you be going back to the airport?
Monica Not just yet. (*Accusingly*) Who's been a naughty boy? (*She brandishes a large salami, and he chokes on his drink*)
Fisher (*guiltily*) When?

Monica takes a modest posy of flowers from her shopping basket, holds it up

Monica Look!
Fisher Oh, f ... f ... flowers!
Monica You're naughty! *I* should be giving flowers to the birthday boy. I bumped into the man from the flower shop and he gave them to me. They're beautiful. You shouldn't.

Monica kisses him. He draws her close and her head is over his shoulder, facing the audience. He tries, surreptitiously, to get the card all the time during the ensuing scene

Fisher Why not, my little "Mini Moke"? Absence makes the heart grow "Honda".

A look of acute pain crosses Monica's face, indicating that she is allergic to his jokes

Monica That was lovely, Peter! You should add that to your list of jolly jokes.
Fisher (*modestly*) I have. (*He gestures to the flowers*) I thought about a big bunch of orchids, but these are small enough to take on the plane. Give them to your folks. They'll brighten up the vicarage.
Monica It's a lovely thought, Peterkins.
Fisher Shall I put them in water for you?

Fisher grabs at the card with the flowers, but Monica manages to hang on to them

Monica No! I want to see what my Peterkins has said to his Moo-Moo.
Fisher Don't strain your eyes, I'll tell you. (*He tries to grab the card but fails*)
Monica If you wanted to tell me, you wouldn't have bothered to enclose a card, would you? (*She holds the card up and reads aloud*) "This is goodbye, but thank you for a wonderful experience. I know it'll hurt for a while, but I'm sure it is better and cleaner this way. Peter."

Monica looks at him. He smiles weakly

Fisher Not very original I'm afraid, but it came from the heart.
Monica "This is goodbye"?
Fisher Sorry? I don't understand.
Monica Neither do I. What on earth does this message mean?
Fisher (*temporizing*) Doesn't it speak for itself?
Monica Not to me it doesn't.
Fisher You're leaving. I'm just saying "good-bye".

Monica Sounds like a suicide note!
Fisher That's how I feel when you go away.
Monica After all these years? You sentimental old thing!

Monica moves towards the kitchen door, taking the flowers and her shopping bag. Fisher utters an audible sigh of relief. Then Monica stops and turns

   What will hurt?
Fisher Hurt? (*He pats his heart*) The old ticker, my darling. It gets that awful "going-back-to-school" feeling when you leave.
Monica (*touched*) Aaaah! (*She turns to go and stops again*) Peter, I'm still a bit puzzled. What "wonderful experience" are you talking about?
Fisher Well, you know—us, together.
Monica When?
Fisher Oh, come on, my little "Alpine". Guess!
Monica (*wracking her brains*) Alp ... Kitzbuhel?
Fisher Got it in one!
Monica But that was our honeymoon.
Fisher (*sexily*) Yes. Do you remember what I whispered in your ear as we lay close on the ski slopes?
Monica Vividly. It was some terrible joke about snowballs.
Fisher (*laughing*) Good Lord! I'd completely forgotten that one.
Monica I wish I had. I'll just pop these things into the kitchen.

The telephone rings. Fisher picks up the receiver

   Monica exits to the kitchen

Fisher (*on the phone*) Fisher. ... Oh, hello Charlie! How are things with Midland Motors in Hamburg? ... Really? Same sad story here, but at least you bachelors have all those strip joints to wile away the boring hours. ... No, Monica hasn't gone yet. Her plane was delayed. We're on our way now. So what can I do for you? ... You're sending me a present? That's very nice of you. I never remember your birthday. What is it? ... Oh, come on! Give me a clue. ... Arriving this morning, and it's three nine, two six, three six?

   Monica enters as Peter says the numbers

   God! Another code to remember. ... (*He sees Monica*) Must fly, Charlie, a little bird's just flown in. ... Bless your heart, me old luv. (*He hangs up*) That was dear old Charlie from Hamburg.
Monica Was that somebody's telephone number Charlie was giving you?
Fisher Telephone number?
Monica Thirty-nine, twenty-six, thirty-six.
Fisher Oh, that? No, some stupid clue about a birthday present which is arriving this morning.
Monica Well, he can afford to buy presents, can't he? He does occasionally sell a car.
Fisher Steady my little "Thunderbird". Do I detect a slight touch of the bitters? Business has increased a hundred percent this year.

Monica A hundred percent of one is still only two. (*She goes to open the front door*)

Fisher But it's a start. Shall I drop you at the airport?

Monica No. Just help me to the lift, and Kurt can grab me a cab outside. Now, Peter, you will promise me that you'll eat properly while I'm away. You never eat enough.

Fisher It's all right, I've got boxes and boxes of stuff in the kitchen.

Monica Yes, and they all say "whisky" on the label. I mean *eat* properly.

Fisher picks up Monica's vanity case and goes to the door with it, leaving her to cope with the suitcase

Peter!

Fisher Oh, sorry darling. Let me hump it for you.

Monica goes out of the front door

Fisher goes to the suitcase and attempts to lift it. It is very heavy. He is caught off balance and it falls down the two steps with him

Monica re-appears at the door from the hall

Monica Quickly, darling, the lift's here!

Fisher Moo-Moo, what have you got in here?

Monica Only a few dresses.

Fisher You might have taken them out of the wardrobe first.

They both exit into the hall with "good-byes". Fisher re-appears

Good-bye, darling.

Monica (*off*) Good-bye, darling!

Fisher (*yelling after her*) Give my love to your mother. (*Then, to himself*) With a mallet.

He closes the front door, hurries to the filing cabinet. He opens drawer 2, takes out the book and papers, and closes it. As he walks down to the sofa, drawer 1 opens slowly. The front doorbell rings. He walks nervously to the door, and notices the drawer is open, so he closes drawer 1. Drawer 2 opens slowly. Fisher closes drawer 2. Drawer 1 opens fast and hits him on the head. Fisher closes drawer 1. Simultaneously drawer 4 opens fast and gets him on the shin. He kicks it shut and then hobbles to open the door

Cadwallader, a man of middle age, stands outside in a sombre city suit and bowler hat. He sports a military moustache and carries a briefcase

Cadwallader Mr Fisher?

Fisher Yes?

Cadwallader clears his throat portentously

Cadwallader I've—come—about—a—car.

Fisher (*pleasantly surprised*) Good God . . . Good-morning. Come in.

Cadwallader enters. Fisher closes the door and joins him

So, sir, you want a car?

Cadwallader No.

Fisher Sorry, I could have sworn you said you'd come about a car.

Cadwallader I did.

Fisher But you don't want a car?

Cadwallader No.

Cadwallader's face suffers a twitch. Fisher gives a start and moves back nervously

Fisher So may I ask what you do want?

Cadwallader (*deliberately*) I've come about a car.

Fisher (*blank*) Oh Lord!

Cadwallader's eyes narrow. If possible, his face looks grimmer

Cadwallader Repeat. "I've come about a car."

Fisher Oh, all right. "I've come about a car."

Cadwallader (*yelling*) No! You're not supposed to repeat that.

Fisher You just told me to.

Cadwallader We may have got off on the wrong foot. Forget this ever happened.

Cadwallader turns and walks smartly out of the front door and slams it

Fisher They should never have let him out.

The front doorbell rings. Fisher opens the door

Cadwallader stands outside

Cadwallader Good-morning. "I've come about a car."

Fisher What, again?

Cadwallader No! No! Wrong! You haven't seen me before.

Fisher I was hoping I'd never see you again.

Cadwallader Come here. I'll give you one more chance. Now think! "I've come about a car." And you say ...? (*He waits, looking hopefully at Fisher*)

Fisher (*hesitantly*) "No, you haven't"?

Cadwallader NO!

Fisher I give up.

Cadwallader (*a snarl*) Oh, do you?

Fisher Yes, well, thank you very much for coming. I won't keep you any longer. Your ambulance must be waiting.

Cadwallader Of course you've never heard of BSI?

Fisher (*hoarsely*) British Security of Industry?

Cadwallader Yes.

Fisher I may have. (*Suavely, à la Bond*) Something to do with industrial espionage, but I really wouldn't know. I'm just in the old motor trade, aren't I?

Cadwallader (*gripping Fisher by his lapels*) Do you deny that you are a BSI agent?

Fisher (*a jump ahead*) Oh no, you don't catch me like that, squire—not an old campaigner like yours truly! I didn't get where I am today falling for a trap like that, Sunny Jim. I don't open *my* trap until I get the correct password.

Cadwallader You've had the correct password a dozen times! "I've come about——"

Fisher (*realizing*) "—a car"!

Cadwallader Yes! To which you should have replied, "I have just the model for you".

Fisher Oh, sorry. "I have just the model for you."

Cadwallader Didn't you decode your instructions?

Fisher Well—to be honest, I got a bit behind and I was starting to decode it only a few minutes ago.

Cadwallader How far did you get?

Fisher "Dear Fisher, Operation imminent."

Cadwallader Oh, well done!

Fisher But I do remember last week's message. It was a bit vague, but it said there was a senior agent from Intelligence Headquarters coming here one day this week.

Cadwallader It wasn't vague at all. It said Monday, not "one day". *Monday* this week.

Fisher Oh, silly me! Then that's today—roughly.

Cadwallader Not roughly—precisely. Where did they dig you up? We don't expect genius, but we do look for a modicum of intelligence.

Fisher Oh, I think I can manage a modicum.

Cadwallader Don't you know there's a war on?

Fisher (*shocked*) Good Lord! There was nothing on the news this morning ...

Cadwallader Not a shooting war. I mean a war on the industrial front. Forget about military intelligence, your James Bonds and Smiley's People. Chaps like us—we are the new élite.

Fisher I say! Are we really?

Cadwallader So you should walk tall and be proud of what you're doing.

Fisher I am. Rely on me. I'm tougher than I look. (*He gives Cadwallader's chest a hard, friendly thump. He then turns quietly pale, as he nurses very bruised knuckles after hitting something very hard*) What've you got under there?

Cadwallader Something I rely on a lot more than I do you. (*He produces a gun and shows it before replacing it*)

Fisher You haven't seen me in a tight corner yet. I've done the course, you know. (*He demonstrates with a string of athletic movements which involve karate chops and Thai boxing. He finally goes to lean casually on the back of the sofa, misses it, falls and disappears from sight. He re-appears shamefaced*) That was the Suma Sofa fall.

Cadwallader I still prefer this. (*He taps his chest*) Did you read last week's instructions carefully?

Fisher Absolutely. To the letter. Know them by heart. But just refresh my memory.

Cadwallader Since your apartment is the nearest to the Berlin Wall, it is to be the rendezvous for an important visitor, coming over the Wall from the East.

Fisher It may seem a stupid question but surely the Wall isn't there any more.

Cadwallader (*impatiently*) Just a figure of speech. Actually, he'll be coming *under*, using a tunnel.

Fisher Why? When all he has to do is walk straight through.

Cadwallader Because that's the way he prefers it! So stop asking stupid questions. We are calling it "Operation Hans".

Fisher Oh course. I remember reading that in the instructions.

Cadwallader No, you don't. It wasn't in the instructions.

Fisher (*quickly*) Correct. Just checking. (*He gives Cadwallader a condescending pat*) Well done! Carry on.

Cadwallader (*acidly*) Thank you. Hans will be bringing us details of the most amazing and revolutionary discovery since the harnessing of nuclear power, which is why the apartment has got to be empty.

Fisher Oh, it is. I mean, it will be. I hope. (*He moves to the drinks table*)

Cadwallader There's no room for hope in our game, Fisher. The apartment *will* be empty, or you're for the high jump. If the Russians get wind of this meeting they'll blow this building and everybody in it to Kingdom come.

Fisher nervously squirts soda from the siphon on to the carpet

Fisher (*hiding his nerves*) Would you join me in a drink?

Cadwallader (*nodding*) Gin.

Fisher I'll try to get yours in the glass. (*Pouring drinks*) I must say, sir, that it's not been easy combining my work with Midland Motors and BSI.

Cadwallader I hear rumours that Midland Motors are in trouble.

Fisher No. Just a minor gearbox fault with the new Cyclone. I'm expecting a Rep any time now with details of modifications. They're not in any trouble.

Cadwallader Hope you're right.

Fisher Thank you and, by the way, thanks a lot for being so understanding about the decoding. I'm damned lucky. You could have been that monster hatchet man of theirs.

Cadwallader Who would that be?

Fisher You must know him. Everyone says he's a psycho, a real nut-case. He's got a terrible twitch. What's his name — *Wallader!*

Cadwallader You mean Cadwallader.

Fisher No! Cadwallader? (*He chuckles*) I never realized; always thought they were talking about "that frightful cad Wallader"! (*He laughs*) Anyway ... (*he proffers the glass*) ... what's your name?

Cadwallader Cadwallader.

Fisher's hand jerks convulsively and he hurls the contents of the glass into the air. He quickly recovers poise

Fisher What a coincidence! Any relation?

Cadwallader merely glares

Have another drink? The old Beefeater, wasn't it? (*He pours another drink*) Have you come straight from London?

Cadwallader No, Bremen.

Fisher Old Tubby Fanshaw is our BSI agent there, isn't he?

Cadwallader goes for his gun

Cadwallader You're not supposed to know that.

Fisher leaps at Cadwallader and pulls his hand away from the gun

Fisher Don't panic.

During the ensuing speech Fisher carefully unclenches Cadwallader's fingers, slides his hand into his right-hand jacket pocket. He then buttons up the jacket into the wrong buttonhole, giving the jacket a lopsided look

Tubby being in the motor trade, too, we foregather from time to time. Got a bit pi ... pi ... plastered one night and it all came out. But don't worry. We haven't told anyone else. (*He tries to straighten the jacket, patting it and jerking it but finally gives up*) You must give me the address of your tailor some time. (*He then goes back to the drinks table*) How is old Tubby? How is the old reprobate?

Cadwallader Gone.

Fisher finishes pouring the drink

Fisher Oh? Retired? Back to the UK?

Cadwallader No, he was shot.

Fisher's drink shoots into the air again, and he manages to catch some of it

Fisher (*enquiringly*) Er—how? Was it suicide—or——?

Cadwallader (*tapping his hidden gun*) No comment.

Fisher thrusts the half empty glass into Cadwallader's hand

Fisher Hang on to that. Try not to spill it this time. (*He goes to pour himself a drink*) I'm really sorry to hear that. I liked old Tubby. We had some good times together. What was his problem?

Cadwallader He was a married man but got sexually involved with a stripper from Hamburg.

Fisher (*with a guilty start*) Hamburg!

Cadwallader Some tart with a loud mouth and a big bust.

Fisher (*sudden realization*) That's Charlie ... thirty-nine ... twenty-six ...

Cadwallader What?

Fisher Goodness me! Look at the time! It's thirty-nine, twenty-six. (*He takes Cadwallader's glass, looks at his watch and in so doing inadvertently pours the contents of Cadwallader's glass into his own empty glass. He quickly drinks the contents and gives a little shudder*) Well, you'd better be going now. She'll be ... I mean, you'll be wanting to beetle off and book in somewhere.

Cadwallader I'm staying here. The deadline is any time after midday.

Fisher Oh, my God!

Cadwallader perches on the desk with his seat near the speaker of the intercom, which suddenly gives voice very loudly, causing him to jump up

Kurt's Voice Bitte! Herr Fisher. Are you there?

Fisher flips the "On" switch

Fisher Yes?

Kurt's Voice Kurt from the showroom calling Herr Fisher.

Fisher Yes, I know who you are. What do you want?

Kurt's Voice I am going now for my lunch in ten minutes.

Fisher Oh, you're back from coffee then? Guten appetit.

Kurt's Voice Danke, and do you want I am bringing back a tart for you?

Fisher Not today, thank you. (*He flips the "Off" switch*) That's my assistant
   in the showroom. And when he says tart, he doesn't mean tart. He . . .

Cadwallader (*sharply*) He'd better not. Can he overhear what goes on in this
   room?

Fisher Only when this switch is on. Look here, sir, I suggest you take a
   walk.

Cadwallader Why?

Fisher I don't like the look of you.

Cadwallader I don't like the look of you, either, but for the present we're
   stuck with each other.

Fisher No, I meant you don't look yourself. Why not go for a stroll down
   the Kurfurstendamm and bring a bit of colour to your cheeks? (*He opens
   the front door*)

Cadwallader (*opening the kitchen door; closing it*) No thanks. I tell you
   where I would like to go.

Fisher Anywhere! Just say the word and I'll direct you.

Cadwallader (*opening the cupboard door and closing it*) Your lavatory.

Fisher (*clutching at straws*) That's not my lavatory. That's my cupboard.
   I've got a better idea. There's a marvellous new public convenience on the
   corner of Kaiserdamm and Charlottenstrasse . . .

*Fisher starts to push Cadwallader through the front door. Cadwallader resists.
The door remains ajar*

Cadwallader I don't want to go to a public lavatory!

Fisher You mustn't miss this one. Pilgrims come from all over the world to
   see it. Magnificent—a symphony in pink and grey with the most tasteful
   mosaics in the shape of a target . . .

Cadwallader I am not interested in public lavatories. (*He looks at him
   sharply*) And I hope you aren't. Where is it?

Fisher I told you, at the corner of Kaiser——

Cadwallader The one here!

Fisher Oh, the one here is there. (*He points*) But I've bad news about that
   lavatory.

Cadwallader I don't want news about it. I just want to use it.

   Cadwallader exits UL

Fisher (*calling after him*) On your own head be it! It's got a dodgy cistern.

   Heidi enters round the front door and starts to caress Fisher

Heidi Peter, darling, what is keeping you? Now we only have one and a half
   hours until Otto comes back.

Fisher Not now, Heidi. The doctor's here. I'm having a check-up.

Heidi I can't think why.

Cadwallader (*off*) Fisher!

Fisher That's him! The doctor! He mustn't see you, he'll say you're bad for my heart.

Fisher pushes Heidi out of the door, leaving her handbag on his arm

Cadwallader enters and reacts to seeing Fisher casually swinging a handbag

Cadwallader Is that someone at the door?

Fisher (*involuntarily*) Wrong knockers.

Cadwallader accepts this and exits again

Fisher opens the door and gives the bag to Heidi, both say "Danke"

Heidi exits

Fisher hurries to the desk and flips the "On" switch

Kurt!

Kurt's Voice Bitte?

Fisher Thank heaven you're still there! Now listen carefully. There is a young lady from Hamburg ...

Kurt's Voice Aha! I don't think I know this one. I hope it is as good as "There was a young lady von Buckingham ..."

Fisher Shut up! This is a Red Alert, Kurt. I'm expecting a young lady to arrive. If she comes in your way, head her off. It's a matter of life and death.

Kurt's Voice Why? Has your wife come back?

Fisher No, and don't even mention things like that. Tell the lady I'm out and will contact her later. Oh, and get her address.

Kurt's Voice Ja. What size?

Fisher Oh God! Where she's living.

Kurt's Voice I don't know where she's living. Where *is* she living?

Fisher I don't know! That's why I want you to get her address.

Pause

Have you got it?

Kurt's Voice Oh come on, do you think I'm Superman or something? How can I get it so quick? I am not going out yet.

Fisher Oh, forget it!

Fisher flips the "Off" switch. The front doorbell rings, and the phone rings simultaneously. He dithers between the two, and answers the front door first

Outside stands a masculine-looking figure in crash helmet, goggles and overalls, with a paper in one hand

Kommen sie in. Ich musta ze telefunken maken.

Fisher runs to answer the telephone and answers it with his back to the front door. The figure enters and swiftly removes crash helmet, goggles and overalls to reveal Mitzi, a gorgeous Juno-esque creature dressed in black stockings, suspenders and a sexy corselet. She tosses her gear behind the hatstand, then moves DC, *getting ready to sing*

(*On the phone*) Hello. . . . Oh, Charlie. . . . No, nothing has arrived, but I know what that "nothing" is and I could murder you. If I don't head her off, I'm in the——

Mitzi sings Happy Birthday. Fisher turns and sees her. He gives a great start and, unthinkingly, shoves the telephone in his trouser pocket. He rushes across and puts a hand over her mouth. He then removes the telephone from his pocket

(*On the phone*) It's no good shouting. I'm deaf in that pocket.

Fisher replaces the phone. Mitzi starts to sing again. Fisher rushes back to her

Quiet! Please!
Cadwallader (*off*) Fisher!

Fisher pushes Mitzi on to the couch

Fisher That is him! Now lie down on this settee . . .
Mitzi Look, I know it's your birthday but can't we have a chat first?
Fisher No, I don't mean that. Just lie there and don't say anything until I speak to you.

Fisher covers Mitzi with cushions

Cadwallader enters UL

Fisher immediately runs up and starts to mask him from the sofa, by clasping his hands behind his head

You called?
Cadwallader There's nothing wrong in that lavatory.
Fisher Who said there was?
Cadwallader You did.

Now Cadwallader dodges past him and starts to circle the room with Fisher still using himself as a shield between Cadwallader and the sofa

Fisher Did I?
Cadwallader Yes, you said you had bad news in there.
Fisher That's right. I was in there when the bad news came.
Cadwallader What bad news?
Fisher I'd rather not discuss it. It's still very painful.
Cadwallader (*shaking his head*) There's something very fishy.
Fisher In the loo?
Cadwallader About you. The way you're carrying on. If you're trying to hide something from me I shall find it. I've eyes in the back of my head.

Fisher quickly puts his hand behind Cadwallader's head

Fisher Hiding something? What on earth would I want to hide from you?
Cadwallader I don't know—yet. But I suggest you give me the answer to a few pertinent questions. What goes on in the public convenience in Charlottenstrasse? Why did you want me there? What is it about the lavatory here? Why didn't you want me to go in there? Why do you jump guiltily at half the things I say?

They have now moved quite a way from the sofa and Fisher relaxes a little

And Fisher?
Fisher Yes?
Cadwallader One other minor matter you may care to explain.
Fisher Pleasure, sir, what?
Cadwallader What is that woman doing on the sofa?

Fisher looks at the sofa and then back at Cadwallader

Fisher Nothing very much. Just lying there. (*He takes Cadwallader's arm*)
Cadwallader Who is she?
Fisher A very pertinent question.
Cadwallader And the answer had better be your wife.
Fisher (*relieved*) Brilliant. Yes! Of course it is. Who else?

On the sofa, Mitzi looks astonished at this, but says nothing. She sits up as Fisher leads Cadwallader back to her

Now let me introduce you. This is my wife ... M ... er ...
Mitzi Mitzi.
Fisher Mitzi! Yes, my dear old dutch. Just back from her old-time dancing class. She's a vicar's daughter, believe it or not.

Cadwallader is eyeing Mitzi broodingly

Cadwallader Yes, I know. I am fully cognizant of your lady wife's background. (*To Mitzi*) Mitzi, eh?
Mitzi That's right.
Cadwallader I thought your name was Monica?
Fisher It was: but she has another moniker now. It's Mitzi—for short.
Cadwallader How do you do?
Mitzi Very well, thank you.
Fisher My love, I'd like you to meet a most important gentleman from BSI.
Cadwallader (*tempted to throttle him*) Fool!
Fisher (*smoothly changing gear*) And BSI, as you may have guessed, stands for British Sanitary Inspector.
Cadwallader (*mollified*) First class!
Fisher I do beg your pardon. (*To Mitzi*) In this case British Sanitary Inspector, *First Class*.
Mitzi Then what's he doing here?

Fisher He's been sent here on a course, and he's fixed us with new washers on all the taps. (*He turns to Cadwallader and slips him a tip*) Thanks for your trouble, Mr Fawcet. (*He tries to lead Cadwallader towards the door*) Nice of you to drop by. My regards to Mrs Fawcet and all the little drips—drippers—nippers . . .

Cadwallader resists being shoved out and pushes Fisher away

Cadwallader I am not leaving until I have made a *certain connection*. And I'd like a word with you in private . . . (*hating this*) Sir!

Fisher Oh? Mopsy, darling, pop into the kitchen and make us a cup of coffee.

Fisher has moved close to Mitzi and contrives to make conspiratorial faces at her

Mitzi (*at a loss*) The kitchen?

Fisher (*gesturing vaguely* R) Yes, where you run me up all those delicious meals. (*To Cadwallader*) She spoils me. (*To Mitzi*) Hop along, Moosie, and shut the door.

Mitzi moves R and walks straight into the walk-in cupboard before the horrified Fisher can stop her, and shuts the door. Some crashes are heard

Cadwallader registers this. He looks at Fisher and his face twitches. Fisher gives him a smile and whistles casually. Quite a long pause, then there is a knock on the cupboard door

(*Blandly*) Come out!

Mitzi comes out of the cupboard, looking sheepish

Fisher now surreptitiously indicates the kitchen door

Mitzi exits into the kitchen closing the door

Cadwallader Fisher——?

Fisher (*cutting in*) And you may well ask why Mumsie walked into that cupboard.

Cadwallader Why did Mumsie walk into that cupboard?

Fisher You may well ask.

Cadwallader I did.

Fisher She's as blind as a bat without her glasses, and this is her first day without them on—in. Either that, or she's got them on the wrong way round.

Cadwallader You're talking gibberish.

Fisher No! It's her new contact lenses. She's going through hell with them.

Cadwallader I don't know why I'm bothering with trivialities like that, anyway.

Fisher I don't either.

Cadwallader Because you're a dead man, Fisher. Tubby Fanshaw's transgression with his stripper was peanuts compared to this.

Fisher She's not a stripper! She's my wife. You said so yourself.

Cadwallader If you had read your instructions you'd have known you had to get rid of your wife.
Fisher Murder her?
Cadwallader No, you dolt! Get her out of Berlin during Operation Hans. Her presence here is a disaster. Disaster!
Fisher Oh, you can trust old Mimsie.
Cadwallader What do you mean, trust? (*He seizes him by the lapels*) I warn you, Fisher, if she overheard what went on, you are through — finished — as sure as my name is Walter Cadwallader.
Fisher No, no! She couldn't overhear. She couldn't.
Cadwallader Couldn't? She's not deaf is she?
Fisher (*clutching at straws*) You noticed! Deaf as a post.
Cadwallader But you said she was as blind as a bat.
Fisher And deaf. A tragic fishing accident.
Cadwallader But she answers when you speak to her.
Fisher Lip-reading. Didn't you notice how I put my face close to hers?
Cadwallader (*delayed take*) Fishing . . .? How do you go deaf after a fishing accident?
Fisher Please! I don't want to talk about it. Look, sir, problem solved! I will get rid of her like you said. I can have her out of the flat and on her bike in five minutes . . .
Cadwallader No. I can't take risks. She may not leave the flat or use the phone. I warn you I have a man outside with orders forcibly to detain anyone who causes me problems. Just going to make a private call from your bedroom.

Fisher indicates the phone

No, I don't trust that intercom.

Cadwallader exits UL

Heidi runs in through the windows. She now wears a shortie bathrobe and the smallest of bikinis

Heidi Peter, what is happening? Now we only have one hour left.
Fisher Not now, darling!
Cadwallader (*off*) Fisher! Briefcase!
Fisher It's him!

Fisher utters a gasp and hurls Heidi on to the middle of the sofa. He gets on to the L end of the sofa and hastily pulls a rug over them. Heidi is completely hidden and so is Fisher's lower half

Cadwallader enters

Fisher leans back casually as if taking a rest; but now something starts to happen under the rug which causes his face to twitch convulsively. He shifts about, trying not to give anything away. He lifts the rug briefly and darts an accusing look in Heidi's direction. Cadwallader watches all this, puzzled

Cadwallader What are you doing under that rug?

Fisher Nothing much. Just stretching my legs.

As Fisher says this, Heidi's legs stretch out of the R end of the sofa, thus giving Fisher the appearance of having an incredibly long body—and high-heeled shoes. Cadwallader's attention is distracted by the ringing of the telephone

Cadwallader Could be for me. I'll take it in there.

Cadwallader exits UL *again*

Fisher grabs Heidi's hand and drags her towards the front door

Heidi Who was that?
Fisher A private detective, hired by my wife to spy on you and me. So you must keep away.
Heidi But, Peter, I want to be with you . . .
Fisher Yes, Heidi, later, later . . .

Fisher pushes her out of the front door and slams it

Heidi exits

Mitzi enters from the kitchen

Mitzi Excuse me . . .?
Fisher (*whirling round*) Oh no! Not another one!
Mitzi Look, you do realize I'm Charlie's birthday present from Hamburg . . .? I've got a job here in Berlin, so Charlie . . .

Fisher, scared, looks UR

Fisher Yes, yes. Keep it down if you don't mind.
Mitzi Have I called at an awkward moment?
Fisher More awkward than you know, Miss . . . um . . .
Mitzi Mitzi. Mitzi von Zeppelin.
Fisher Miss von Zeppelin, I'm terribly sorry you've been dragged into this.
Mitzi (*with a philosophic shrug*) C'est la vie.
Fisher I must say you speak remarkably good English.
Mitzi (*laughing*) I should hope so. I was born in Streatham.
Fisher Oh! Your father or grandfather was a Zeppelin?
Mitzi No. It's just my stage name—von Zeppelin. Well, I must fly.
Fisher You'll have to stay here.
Mitzi I can't. I've got a big show tonight for a whole crowd of Japanese and their cameras. I'm a dancer.
Fisher Ballet or modern?
Mitzi Well, sort of in between—a stripper.
Fisher (*poleaxed*) Stripper!
Mitzi If you'd like another birthday present, come along and see the show. It's ever so rude.
Fisher I'm sorry, but you're not permitted to leave.
Mitzi Who says so?
Fisher Him, the big—Sanitary Inspector.
Mitzi Stuff him for a start. What's it got to do with a Sanitary Inspector?

Fisher Nothing.

Mitzi (*preparing to leave*) All right then.

Fisher No, Mimsie, I'll explain. (*He lowers his voice*) He isn't a Sanitary Inspector. He's the head of Berlin's vice squad and he's requisitioned this flat.

Mitzi (*alarmed*) Oh crumbs! Then the sooner I get out the better.

Fisher (*grabbing her again*) No! What is the name of the club where you're stripping off tonight?

Mitzi The Kammerspilergrossekleinestachelschweinegrippenhause.

Fisher Oh no! The Stacher—Stashy—. . . thingy. It was on the tip of my tongue. He's leading a raid on it and other joints tonight. It's five years for all concerned.

Mitzi Five years!

Fisher And nothing off for strippers.

Mitzi Then I can't even go back to my digs. They're right over the club.

Fisher (*pleased*) You certainly can't. That settles it. You're my wife and you're staying here. It's the only way to save you.

Mitzi Thanks, but I'd better phone the club and warn them.

Fisher No, that's verboten.

Mitzi Why?

Fisher Mr Fawcet has tapped all the phones in the neighbourhood. Now, if you're going to pretend to be my wife, I'd better fill you in on some background info.

Mitzi Yes, you'd better!

Fisher Memorize these facts carefully. Your maiden name was Ruddle. Your father, Christian name John, is vicar of St Thomas's, Cheltenham.

Mitzi (*memorizing hard*) John . . . Thomas . . . Cheltenham . . . (*She roars with laughter*) John . . . Thomas . . .

Fisher Sh! Please, try to remember that you were educated at Cheltenham Ladies College. (*To himself*) I'm never going to get away with this. (*To Mitzi*) Later you became a very successful horse-woman and show jumper. So much so that our bedroom here is littered with your silver trophies.

Cadwallader enters UL. *He approaches Mitzi, thrusts his face close to hers, mouths his words and mimes a cup with his hands*

Cadwallader I hope you don't object, but I've been admiring your cups, Mrs Fisher.

Mitzi is proud of her statistics, and hitches up her bra

Mitzi Thirty-nine.

Cadwallader Much more and they won't go on the mantelpiece. You must be one of the fastest girls in the show—under forty seconds, eh?

Mitzi Ooh, it's much faster than that with a good crowd egging you on. It's Velcro, you see, and one good pull can . . .

Fisher (*leaping in*) HICKSTEAD! Mr Faucet is talking about all the cups you won *show-jumping*, riding dear old Velcro.

Mitzi Oh! Oh, yes.
Cadwallader How many hands?
Mitzi Two—well, only one when I'm using the whip.

Cadwallader gives up

Cadwallader (*to Fisher*) Doesn't lip-read very well, does she?

Cadwallader again perches on the desk near the intercom speaker. Kurt's voice suddenly blares forth, causing Cadwallader to jump

Kurt's Voice Bitte! Kurt from showroom calling Herr Fisher.

Fisher moves across, flips the "On" switch

Fisher Yes, Kurt?
Kurt's Voice I think you will be very pleased with me.
Fisher I hope so. What about?
Kurt's Voice I have bought for you two very pretty dresses and a knitted skirt.

Fisher looks embarrassed. Cadwallder gives Fisher a look

One blue, one red and . . .
Fisher To hell with the colour. Take them back.
Kurt's Voice You don't want dresses any more?
Fisher I don't want dresses and I don't want a skirt, Kurt. I'm busy. Anything else?
Kurt's Voice Ja. I am having two very mysterious phone messages about some singing nightingale from der East.
Cadwallader (*hoarsely—seizing the intercom*) Repeat that! Exact wording!
Kurt's Voice What has happened to your voice, Herr Fisher? You have a toad in your throat?
Fisher No, I haven't. Just repeat as he said . . . as I said . . . what they said.
Cadwallader (*in a loud whisper*) About the nightingale.
Fisher About the nightingale.
Kurt's Voice Now you are having an echo. Twice a man calls and says "The nightingale from the East has taken wing and will sing".
Cadwallader (*in a low voice to Fisher*) Those calls should be coming up here. Someone in London has blundered.
Fisher (*to the intercom*) Kurt, if you get any more calls like that, you put them straight through up here.
Kurt's Voice Ja. Over and aus.

Fisher flips the "Off" switch. Cadwallader clearly wants to get rid of Mitzi

Cadwallader Do you think you could ask your wife if that coffee is ready yet?
Fisher Of course. So sorry. (*Then mouthing*) Coffee, Mimsie.
Mitzi I can't find it.
Fisher On the shelf where it always is.
Mitzi I've got that. I can't find the stove.

Cadwallader What!?

Fisher (*apologizing, sotto voce*) The memory's not too good, either. (*Then normally*) Anything else you'd like?

Cadwallader Well, I'm pretty peckish; wouldn't mind an omelette.

Fisher Did you hear that, Mopsy? (*Hastily*) No, of course you didn't. (*Mouthing into her face*) One omelette.

Cadwallader moves out on to the balcony

Mitzi I've never cooked an omelette.

Fisher Never mind. Find a cookery book and look it up.

Mitzi OK. (*She starts to go, stops*) How do you spell it?

Fisher (*doesn't know*) O double M ... No, O, E, M ... Oh, look the damned thing up under "eggs".

Mitzi exits into the kitchen

Cadwallader re-enters from the balcony

Cadwallader That message means that Hans is on his way with the goods. Tremendous!

Fisher Super!

Cadwallader How many ways are there up to the roof?

Fisher Either through the front door and up the staircase or through the french windows and up the fire escape.

Cadwallader starts to move away

Excuse me, sir, but if I'm to be a cog in this shouldn't I know more about Hans and what he looks like?

Cadwallader I can't help you there. Nobody knows. He's like a chameleon; a master of disguise. Can dress himself up as anything. Talking of dressing up, why were you ordering women's dresses just now?

Fisher Kurt misunderstood me. It was a slight mistake.

Cadwallader (*giving him a glare*) You'll be making a grave mistake if you go in for that kind of thing. As from this spring, we're giving all transvestites a very short shrift.

Fisher (*straight-faced*) That wouldn't suit me—not with my knees. Sorry. But what is Hans coming up with that's so exciting?

Cadwallader He was on the trail all over Soviet Russia—Siberia, Mongolia—but he finally picked something up deep in the Urals.

Fisher Rotten luck.

Cadwallader And it's ninety-nine per cent certain that he'll give it to us.

Fisher Then we must be jolly careful to wash the teacups thoroughly.

Cadwallader You're a funny fellow, Fisher. I don't understand half the things you say.

Fisher I don't understand anything you say. So what did he pick up in the Urals?

Cadwallader Details of an incredible Russian breakthrough.

Fisher In what?

Cadwallader Imagine a battery, the size of a matchbox, which would drive a large saloon car up to seventy-five miles per hour for one thousand miles without re-charging.
Fisher A thousand miles!
Cadwallader Without re-charging!
Fisher Phew!
Cadwallader Think of our country's industrial gain.
Fisher But what about all the other countries? Aren't they desperate to get their hands on it?
Cadwallader You bet they are, and Russia will be working overtime to get it back. One of the reasons I have an armed sharpshooter on the roof.
Fisher Armed!
Cadwallader I know! But I'm not letting this one go. This is my show. (*He gives a twitch and an evil chuckle*) And one in the eye for the Yankees!
Fisher Yankees? I thought they were on our side.
Cadwallader You're joking. They're ruthless.

A high-pitched bleeper sounds. Cadwallader takes a walkie-talkie from his breast pocket

Acknowledge.

There follows a long, unintelligible, high-pitched metallic gabble. Cadwallader listens intently, occasionally nodding his head. The voice stops

That's very interesting. I'll be right up. Out.

Cadwallader switches off, returns the machine to his breast pocket, turns to Fisher, who clearly hasn't understood a word

Make a note of that, Fisher.
Fisher (*grimacing*) Yes, sir! (*He writes in a notebook*)

Cadwallader exits through the french windows on to the balcony

There is a ring at the front door. Fisher opens it

Heidi stands, still in her bathrobe and bikini

Simultaneously, Mitzi comes out of the kitchen with a frying pan

Mitzi I'm fed up. I can't go on like this ...

Fisher holds Heidi off. She cannot see Mitzi because of the position of the door

Fisher (*to Mitzi*) Not now, dear. Out!

Mitzi hurriedly exits into the kitchen

Heidi (*pushing in and closing the door*) Who is that?
Fisher My old mother. She can't go on much longer. She's just leaving, and so must you.
Heidi Please! I want to be with you. I *have* to be with you!
Fisher No, I know we've only got forty-five minutes, but ...
Heidi It's not that: I think Otto is trying to have me killed.

Fisher Oh, come on, Heidi! He'd never do that.
Heidi I saw a man on the roof. He had a gun!
Fisher No ... I know who that is. That'll be ...
Cadwallader (*off; knocking*) Come on! Let me in!

Fisher immediately pushes Heidi among the hats and coats of the hatstand beside the door. With one movement he arranges a hat over her head and a coat over her body, and her feet are behind a pair of boots, all of which have been there since the rise of the curtain. The knocking is continuous. Fisher opens the door

> *Cadwallader stands there*

Fisher steps back to conceal Heidi

Cadwallader (*angrily*) Didn't you hear me knocking?
Fisher Sorry, I couldn't find the door.

Heidi's arms are through Fisher's so as they appear to be his own. She unbuttons his shirt and caresses his chest. Fisher is doing his best to appear normal

Don't you find it hot in here?
Cadwallader (*ignoring him*) My gunman on the roof has a blind spot. There's another balcony through there, isn't there?
Fisher Yes, off the main bedroom.
Cadwallader Let me see it.

> *Cadwallader exits* UL

Fisher turns to Heidi

Fisher Stay there until I get back.

> *Fisher exits* UL

Heidi comes out from behind the hatstand and heads for the kitchen. The men's voices are heard offstage

> *Heidi hastily dives into the cupboard and shuts the door as*

Fisher and Cadwallader re-enter UL

Cadwallader That's useless. Stand fast, Fisher. I'm going topsides to move that man on the roof.

> *Cadwallader exits through the window and disappears*

Fisher goes to the hatstand and talks to it; at the same time he keeps looking back over his shoulder, making sure Cadwallader doesn't return

Fisher OK, push off now, quickly. Don't hang about.

> *Mitzi comes in from the kitchen and sees Fisher urgently prodding the coats*

Come on, hurry! He'll be back any minute! (*He gets no response, realizes Heidi is not there, turns away relieved*)

Mitzi Do you often talk to hatstands?
Fisher (*put out*) What?
Mitzi Where's that man from the vice squad?
Fisher I hope he's about to fall off the roof.
Mitzi If he's not around, why can't I nip off?
Fisher If you value your life, you'll stay put. How's the omelette?
Mitzi I found the recipe. It says: "Beat the eggs till they break." Well, I beat
them and they broke, but I'll be all day picking out bits of shell.
Fisher No, Mitzi. You have to get the egg out of the shell before you break
it.
Mitzi Oh, pull the other one!
Fisher I mean the inside of the egg out of the shell.
Mitzi (*brightly*) Oh! Make a little hole with a pin and blow it?
Fisher That's one way I suppose. Try it.
Mitzi (*moving*) All right, Mr Fisher.

Mitzi exits into the kitchen

Fisher And please, you're supposed to be my wife. The name is Peter.

The front door opens and Monica enters

Fisher has followed Mitzi and is standing in the kitchen doorway

Monica Peterkins!
Fisher (*without turning*) Funny, that's what my wife calls me.
Monica I bet you're surprised to see me!
Fisher Bloody hell!

*Fisher suddenly realizes that Monica is there. In a flash, he yanks the kitchen
door shut so violently that the handle, plus its attached spindle, comes away in
his hand. He gives Monica a sickly grin, realizes the handle is in his hand.
Monica looks at him*

Monica Have you got a problem?
Fisher Two, actually. Moo-Moo, what are you doing back here? (*He takes
the door-knob and spindle and sticks it furtively back in the door*).
Monica Would you believe it? I've been delayed again. They're having to
change an engine now. I couldn't let you know because there was a queue
a mile long for every phone, so I just hopped in a cab and came back.
Anything exciting happened?
Fisher Not a thing.
Monica Oh, I'm so hot and sticky. I must have a bath. I couldn't even get a
cup of tea at the airport. I'm absolutely parched. (*She moves suddenly
towards the kitchen door*) Would you like one, too?
Fisher (*frantic*) NO!
Monica (*lightly*) "No, thank you". Manners!

Monica exits into the kitchen

*Fisher's shoulders slump. He looks resignedly at his watch and counts out the
seconds aloud*

Fisher One, two, three ... (*On the count of three, like a conjuror, he gestures to the kitchen door*)

Monica promptly enters, closing the door behind her

Monica Peter?
Fisher (*forlornly*) No?
Monica There's a girl in there with her bottom in the air, rubbing egg into the floor.
Fisher No. Rubbing it off, actually.
Monica Why?
Fisher She's making her first omelette.
Monica Why is she making it in our kitchen?
Fisher You sound a wee bit puzzled.
Monica You could say that.
Fisher Remember how you were worried about me not getting enough?
Monica Enough what?
Fisher Food.
Monica Oh, yes?
Fisher Well, by an absolutely amazing coincidence old Helmut Hackman on the third floor has suddenly been called away and asked me if I could use a good plain cook for a couple of months.
Monica Plain? Have you looked at her?
Fisher No.
Monica She's very pretty.
Fisher Is she? (*He opens the kitchen door, peers in, closes it again*) That eagle eye of yours can certainly spot 'em.
Monica I spotted her fancy dress, too.
Fisher No, no, that's not fancy dress. She's just come back from her keep-fit class.
Monica Keeping fit for what?
Fisher Well, it hasn't worked yet. Sad. So sad.
Monica What is?
Fisher She's stone deaf.
Monica Oh no! So young ...
Fisher The result of a tragic accident.
Monica In the kitchen?
Fisher No. Out hunting.
Monica What happened?
Fisher I've no idea.
Monica Didn't you ask her?
Fisher Yes, but she didn't hear a word I said. Care for a drink?

Fisher moves L *towards the drinks. There is a distinct thump from the walk-in cupboard. Monica gives a start and looks scared*

Monica (*whispering*) Did you hear that?
Fisher (*truthfully*) Yes. It was probably the cook.
Monica (*whispering*) I think there's someone in the cupboard.

Fisher No; definitely not.

Monica I tell you, I heard something.

Fisher Could be a mouse.

Monica No, it was too big a thump for a mouse. Go and look.

Fisher You're the boss. (*He moves to the cupboard*) Someone in the cupboard! That's all I need.

He opens the cupboard door and sees Heidi, who cannot be seen by Monica. Fisher rocks slightly and sags at the knees, but quickly recovers his poise. He turns calmly to Monica

You see! Nothing. But I'll just make doubly sure.

He walks purposefully into the cupboard and shuts the door

Monica waits looking faintly puzzled

The cupboard door re-opens and Fisher comes out again almost immediately, closing the door behind him

Yes, you were right. Now what was it you wanted to drink?

Monica Right about what?

Fisher The cupboard. Gin and tonic?

Monica What was it, then—a mouse?

Fisher No. Ice and lemon?

Monica All right. I'll look for myself.

Monica makes a move towards the cupboard. Fisher concedes defeat

Fisher No need. She'll be coming out.

Monica (*stopping, turning*) Who will?

Fisher Heidi, of course.

Monica Heidi?

Fisher Yes. You did say ice?

Monica And why "of course"?

Fisher Well, she can't stay in there all day, can she? (*He pours gin*)

Monica Peter, who is Heidi?

Fisher The maid.

Monica Maid! You'll be saying we've got a butler next!

Fisher digests this, nods to himself and files it away for further use

Fisher I told you old Helmut said I could have his staff.

Monica No, you just told me about Mitzi the cook.

Fisher Yes, and if I took Mitzi the cook, I had to take Heidi the maid. I couldn't have one without the other. They come as a pair.

Monica What is she doing in the cupboard?

Fisher (*promptly*) Spring cleaning.

Monica It's August.

Fisher So it is! Perhaps she doesn't know. She wasn't here in April. (*He goes to open the cupboard door*) Come along now, Heidi. Take a break.

Heidi comes out. She has abandoned her towelling robe and donned a

*pinafore apron purloined from the cupboard. She carries a feather duster.
She curtsies to Fisher and hands him the duster*

(*Accepting the duster as a bunch of flowers*) Thank you. I'll put them in
water.

Heidi Guten tag.

Fisher Ah, Heidi. Let me introduce you to—er—ah ... (*trying to think*) ...
now, who can you be?

Monica What's the matter with you? (*To Heidi*) I am Mrs Fisher.

Fisher Of course you are. Yes, this is my wife Mitzica Fisher—Mrs Fisher.

Monica I'm going to telephone my mother.

Fisher Now Moo-Moo, don't let's be hasty ...

Monica To tell her I'm delayed. And then I shall have a bath.

Monica exits UL

Fisher (*rounding on Heidi*) I thought you'd gone.

Heidi No. I am sorry about your wife.

Fisher So am I, but that is not the point.

Heidi It is a good idea that you make me the maid. Now I can safely stay
here. (*She walks towards the kitchen*)

Fisher (*in a panic*) Where are you going?

Heidi To make you a nice cup of coffee.

Fisher (*in a strangled voice*) No!

Before he can stop her, Heidi enters the kitchen

Fisher sinks on to the sofa, looks at his watch

(*Counting out loud*) One, two, three ... (*He makes the conjuror's gesture
again*)

Heidi returns, shutting the door

Heidi You are not going to tell me that girl in the kitchen is your mother?

Fisher All right, I won't.

Heidi Then who is it?

Fisher A singing telegram girl.

Heidi I want the truth.

Fisher A stripper from Hamburg.

Heidi Don't give me silly answers. Who is she?

Fisher Would you believe Mitzi, a good plain cook?

Heidi You fool! Why did you not tell me?

Fisher Well ... I ... didn't think you would believe me.

Heidi A cook? Would she make me something?

Fisher Well, I don't know, I'll have to ask her. Mitzi!

Mitzi comes out of the kitchen with an egg and a straw

Mitzi Look, I've made the hole and I've tried blowing and sucking, but
nothing comes out.

Fisher Try two holes, and by the way, we need two omelettes now. Medium
rare, sunny side up. Look lively! (*He pushes her back into the kitchen*)

Mitzi exits to the kitchen

Fisher shuts the door after her

Heidi (*adoring*) You are so masterful.
Fisher Got to keep them in their place. Which reminds me, you had better go to the spare room ... (*he points*) ... through there.
Heidi But what am I to do by myself?
Fisher It's got a nice little balcony. Get on with your sunbathing.
Heidi If only you could come too.
Fisher I will. Just give me time.

Heidi kisses him and puts her arms around him

> *Cadwallader comes silently through the window. He looks at them with bulging eyes*

Fisher nervously brings an end to the embrace

> Careful. Someone might come in.

Cadwallader clears his throat raspingly. Fisher stiffens but does not turn round

> Someone has come in.

Fisher turns as Cadwallader walks grimly towards them. Heidi tries a curtsy. Fisher adopts a master/servant voice to Heidi

> You may go, Heidi. Don't forget now, hoover the room and polish your brasses.

> *Heidi curtsies again and exits* DR

> (*To Cadwallader*) Nice girl. Care for a drink?
Cadwallader Who is that?
Fisher (*looking round*) Where?
Cadwallader The woman who is to polish her brasses.
Fisher Oh, *her*? The maid.
Cadwallader (*twitching madly*) A maid!? You never said you had a maid.
Fisher You never asked.
Cadwallader But you were kissing her.
Fisher Yes.
Cadwallader Why?
Fisher It must be obvious. I was comforting the poor creature.
Cadwallader Comforting? She was grinning all over her face.
Fisher Smiling through the tears. She'd just had some very bad news ...
Cadwallader (*gripping him by the lapels*) If it's that lavatory ...
Fisher It is not the lavatory. It was her father. There's been a tragic shooting accident. He was mortally wounded.
Cadwallader Where?

Fisher glances at the picture of the Matterhorn behind the desk

Fisher The Matterhorn.

Cadwallader You climb the Matterhorn. You ski on the Matterhorn, but who goes shooting on the Matterhorn?

Fisher Only a reckless fool.

Cadwallader So she is in mourning?

Fisher The deepest.

Cadwallader This may seem a stupid question, but if she's in mourning, why is she prancing about half naked?

Fisher (*promptly*) Prickly heat.

Cadwallader What?

Fisher Prickly heat. A nervous condition brought on by grief. (*His imagination stretched almost to the limit, he pours himself a majestic drink with a far from steady hand*)

Cadwallader Not very respectful to her father's memory, is it? She looks more like a stripper ...

Fisher No, she's not the stripper. (*He starts indicating the kitchen*) The stripper is ... (*He recovers*) But where are my manners? Have another drink. You look as if you need it.

Cadwallader I need more than a drink. What am I going to say to London? This apartment was supposed to be evacuated—and what do I find? Not one, but *two* potentially dangerous women. Two! What next?

Fisher Nothing, sir, cross my heart ...

Monica sails in UL, *putting dabs of cold cream on her face. She wears an old bathrobe and a flowery bath cap, making her look frumpy*

Monica Peterkins, come and give your Moo-Moo a rub-a-dub in the bathy ...

Fisher chokes on his drink. Cadwallader lets out a howl and leaps up

Cadwallader Aaaaagh!

Monica Aaaaagh! Oh! So sorry! I didn't realize you were ... you had ... (*She starts to retreat*) Oh, I must look a sight. Do forgive me.

Monica hurriedly exits UR *with a nervous laugh*

Fisher Now, where were we?

Cadwallader (*twitching again*) Another stupid question, no doubt, but who the hell was that?

Fisher I already told you ...

Cadwallader (*beginning to jump up and down*) You didn't! You haven't! You never tell me anything!

Fisher (*snapping his fingers*) You're right! I am sorry. I remember now. You were up on the roof when she came home.

Cadwallader Home?

Fisher Yes. She's my wife ... (*hastily*) wife's sister ... er ... Moo-Moo.

Cadwallader (*slowly*) Are—you—telling—me—that—this—Moo-cow lives here too?

Fisher Moo-Moo, not Moo-cow. Yes, always—when she's not in the sanatorium.

Cadwallader Sanatorium?

Fisher (*nodding cheerfully*) Nutty as a fruitcake.

Cadwallader I know I'm not going to like the answer, but what precisely is wrong with her?

Fisher She was dropped on her head.

Cadwallader By her nanny?

Fisher No, by her husband. Frightful man.

Cadwallader When?

Fisher Usually after dinner.

Cadwallader You mean he did it more than once?

Fisher Oh, every day, until the day he died.

Cadwallader Well, his death must have come as a merciful release for her.

Fisher But not for him. (*He shudders, shakes his head*) Ugh!

Cadwallader I have a feeling I shouldn't ask—but how did he die?

Fisher considers this question carefully before replying

Fisher (*at last*) She chopped him up with a meat axe.

Cadwallader What! And she is roaming about—free?

Fisher She only served a year. *Crime passionnel*, they called it.

Cadwallader Even so ... (*He shudders*) A meat axe! Ugh!

Fisher I wouldn't let it worry you. She isn't violent unless you rub her up the wrong way.

Cadwallader Why does she ask you to give her a rub-a-dub in the bath?

Fisher Sex-mad: anything in trousers, but preferably without them. Don't let her ever get you alone.

Cadwallader It's unbelievable—a nightmare! A wife, poor soul, hard of hearing and blind as a bat, who mistakes a cupboard for the kitchen ...

He indicates the kitchen and they both look toward it

A maid half naked with prickly heat ...

They both look DR *through the arch*

And a sex-mad, homicidal, sister-in-law!!

They both turn towards the exit UL

Fisher Apart from that, are you fairly pleased?

Cadwallader grabs Fisher by the throat

CURTAIN

ACT II

The same. The action is continuous

As the CURTAIN *rises, Cadwallader still has Fisher by the throat*

Fisher (*in a throttled voice*) . . . I said are you *fairly* pleased.
Cadwallader Oh yes, I can't wait to be axed to death by a homicidal maniac.

Mitzi enters from the kitchen with a smoking frying pan

Mitzi It's lucky you've got a lot of eggs.
Fisher Why? Are you making a lot of omelettes?
Mitzi No, I'm making a hash of it. Do I have to go on? I keep breaking them.

Cadwallader moves to Mitzi and on the assumption that she is deaf, yells loudly putting his face close to hers

Cadwallader I—expect—it's because—you—put—them—in—the wrong—way—round.
Mitzi (*blankly*) In the frying pan?
Cadwallader No, in your eyes. Your EYES!
Mitzi Eggs in my eyes?
Cadwallader No, not eggs. YOUR CONTACT LENSES!
Mitzi There's no need to shout.
Cadwallader (*reacting, turning to Fisher*) I thought you said she was . . . (*he lowers his voice, spells it out*) . . . D.E.A.F.?
Fisher She L.I.P. reads. I told you—remember?
Cadwallader Oh, yes. That's right, but . . .

Cadwallader, however, remains looking puzzled and is obviously trying to work something out. Fisher pushes Mitzi back to the kitchen, still doing the lip-reading act

Fisher Have another crack at the eggs, darling, and try to break them over the pan.
Mitzi (*almost in tears*) I wish I'd never met you!

Mitzi exits into the kitchen, slamming the door

Fisher Lovers' tiff.
Cadwallader Just a minute. You say your wife only lip-reads?
Fisher Yes.
Cadwallader Then why did she tell me there was no need to shout?
Fisher Well, there wasn't, was there, because she couldn't hear it if you did.

Cadwallader That's my point. If she can't hear, how did she know I was shouting!

Fisher Good question. And one that has puzzled top eye specialists all over the world.

Cadwallader *Eye* specialists?

Fisher Yes.

Cadwallader But we're talking about her ears!

Fisher (*making a smooth recovery after a blink*) Yes. She has such incredibly sharp vision that she can almost hear with her eyes.

Cadwallader But you said earlier on, she was as blind as a bat.

The strain is beginning to tell on Fisher

Fisher Yes.

Cadwallader Well then?

Fisher Have you ever seen two bats collide?

Cadwallader Bats aren't deaf.

Fisher I didn't say they were.

Cadwallader (*beginning to twitch badly*) But you did say she was blind as a bat, without her glasses.

Fisher Why should a bat be wearing her glasses?

Cadwallader I said a bat *without* her glasses.

Fisher Bats don't wear glasses!

Cadwallader I DIDN'T SAY THEY DID!

Fisher Then we agree.

Cadwallader I give up. I shall end up as crazy as the rest of you.

Cadwallader gives a start as his bleeper sounds off. He produces it

(*To the bleeper*) Acknowledge.

Once again the unintelligible voice gives a message—shorter this time

Willco. Out. (*To Fisher*) Did you hear that?

Fisher Nearly all of it.

Cadwallader Better get it down.

As before, Fisher starts to write in a notebook, mumbling the unintelligible message in near perfect imitation of the bleeper

Fisher (*gibberish*) Kark ... Karok ... Yak ... Tic ... Mooligabit ... Comma ... Baruk ... Tok ... Tik ... Millok ... Daba ... Daba ... Blip.

Cadwallader Good man. (*He takes binoculars from his briefcase*)

Cadwallader goes to the window and exits

At the same time, Monica enters UL. *She stops and stares in surprise as Cadwallader disappears*

Monica (*pointing to the window*) Peter, that man just left by the window.

Fisher Yes.

Monica When I came in earlier, I thought he must be a customer.

Fisher Good Lord no! Customers don't leave by the windows.

Monica Then what is he doing out there?

Fisher Watering the flowers.

Monica He hasn't got a watering can.

Fisher My God, you're right. Don't look. It's disgusting.

Monica But who is he?

Fisher Maunders.

Monica Maunders?

Fisher Yes.

Monica Who is Maunders?

Fisher The butler, of course.

Monica Oh come on, Peter, who is he?

Fisher Old Helmut Hackman's butler.

Monica Wh-at! Peter, for ten years we have made do with a daily twice a week.

Fisher Yes.

Monica Now, suddenly, we have a butler, maid and a cook.

Fisher Bit of a change, eh?

Monica And they all work full-time for Helmut Hackman downstairs?

Fisher Of course.

Monica But it's a one-roomed flat!

Fisher No wonder he pushed off . . . (*He embraces her*) God, it's good to have you back. When are you going again?

Monica I've no idea.

Fisher Let me fix you some lunch.

Monica No, you won't.

Fisher No trouble.

Monica You'll do nothing of the kind. I'm not having you skivvying when we're stuffed to the gunwales with staff. It's a crazy situation anyway, but now you've landed us in it, we may as well take advantage and enjoy it. Now you go and get the maid.

Fisher What?

Monica Go and get the maid.

Fisher Oh. Right.

Fisher exits DR

Monica goes to the desk and takes scissors from the drawer, then sits in the desk chair. She is about to cut a loose thread off her dressing gown as . . .

Cadwallader comes back through the window with field glasses. He does not see Monica until he turns and comes face to face with her. He gives a start, eyes the scissors and backs away

Monica Ah, Maunders.

As Monica moves forward, Cadwallader's right hand feels for the gun beneath his jacket

I assume you don't mind if I call you Maunders?

Cadwallader You can call me anything you like as long as you keep your distance.

Monica Now Maunders. If I am to be your mistress I want it to be as pleasant as possible for both of us.

Cadwallader looks terrified. His eyes dart hither and thither for escape routes

Cadwallader (*hoarsely*) Do you?

Monica I'll let you into a little secret. I've never had a butler before.

Cadwallader A butler. Oh, haven't you?

Monica I've had the odd jobbing gardener, of course. And once, when my husband was laid up, I had his chauffeur.

Cadwallader Now, look here . . .

Monica (*laughing*) He was Japanese, you know; quite sweet, very small but jolly willing . . .

Cadwallader Really I . . .

Monica All I had to say was "Chop-chop", and he'd be on the job.

Cadwallader Madam, please!

Monica And so clean! You've never seen anything like it.

Cadwallader And I don't want to, Mrs—er—Miss——

Monica He used to dust everywhere before he'd let me touch anything.

Cadwallader Dear God . . .!

Monica You probably wonder why I'm telling you all this, Maunders.

Cadwallader I do!

Monica It's just that if I can handle a man who hardly spoke a word of English, I'm sure that you and I can make a go of it.

Cadwallader I don't think we should rush into anything . . .

Monica Oh, I do! I've only got a few hours and I want to make the most of them.

Cadwallader (*calling faintly*) Fisher!

Monica And tell me, confidentially, Maunders, what is the longest you have held any one position?

Cadwallader Really! I've never actually—er—timed it. (*He calls louder*) Fisher!

Fisher enters DR

Oh, thank heaven.

Fisher Anything wrong, sir?

Monica Peter! (*To Fisher*) One does not call a butler "sir" and I'm sure Maunders will agree with me.

Cadwallader (*irritated*) Yes . . . I mean, yes, madam. (*He curtsies*)

There is a crash from the kitchen

Monica I'd better go and see what that cook is up to.

Monica moves towards the kitchen. Cadwallader moves close to Fisher and hisses at him

Cadwallader You were right. Mad as a march hare.

Monica opens the kitchen door, pops her head inside. Another crash

Monica Cook, what on earth? (*She stops*) Oh really! Just look at the mess you've made.

Monica exits into the kitchen

Cadwallader (*grabbing Fisher*) Hear that? Now she thinks your wife is the cook. Her own sister!

Fisher Humour her. It's only a game. Today it's "servants and mistresses"—tomorrow it's "doctors and nurses"—much more fun!

Cadwallader I never thought I'd say this to any man, but I may ask you to share my bed tonight.

Fisher I beg your pardon.

Monica enters from the kitchen

Monica Now, where's that maid?

Fisher She's lying down.

Monica Well, what on earth's the matter with the girl?

Cadwallader Prickly heat.

Monica (*severely to Cadwallader*) And you are responsible.

Cadwallader I didn't give it to her! You don't catch prickly heat anyway. You . . . you develop it.

Monica How?

Cadwallader I don't know. I'm an industrial intelligence——

Fisher (*jumping in*) Butler! An industrious, intelligent butler!

Cadwallader Yes. Damn! (*To Fisher*) Thanks.

Monica moves closer to Cadwallader who starts to look petrified. Monica gives Cadwallader a pat

Monica All right, Maunders. Relax, calm down. But before anything else, you and I will decide how best you can serve me. (*To Fisher*) I won't ask you to join in because you're hopeless. (*To Cadwallader*) I must get out of these things. I'll be ready for you in a few minutes.

Cadwallader (*hoarsely*) Ready . . . for what?

Monica To get down to things, but I warn you, if you don't come up to scratch, it's the chop for you.

Cadwallader Oh my God!

Monica turns and exits UL

Mitzi enters from the kitchen with a cookery book

Mitzi Here. It says to add a knob of butter the size of a filbert. What are filberts?

Cadwallader (*impatiently*) Nuts!

Mitzi (*aggrieved*) I wasn't talking to you.

Fisher Mitzi, a filbert is a kind of nut.

Mitzi Oh, I see. (*She giggles*) Silly me!

Mitzi exits into the kitchen

Cadwallader (*suspicious*) Wait a minute! How does she manage to . . .?

At this point Cadwallader's bleeper sounds

(*To bleeper*) Acknowledge.

The bleeper again emits a short, sharp, and still unintelligible message

Understood. Out. (*To Fisher*) Did you get that, Fisher?

Fisher Actually—missed a word or two. Sir.

Cadwallader Someone's just slipped into the building.

Fisher Hans?

Cadwallader Must be. This is the greatest day of my life. Moments like this make you proud to be British. (*He opens the front door and takes up a position to one side of the door, standing to attention*) I think I'll greet him from here.

Fisher Right.

Fisher stands beside Cadwallader who pushes him brusquely behind him

Cadwallader On second thoughts, I think I'll stand over here. (*He moves to the other side of the door*)

Fisher Good thinking.

Fisher joins him—and is once again pushed back

Cadwallader Stand to attention now.

Fisher Yes sir.

They both stand erect and wait

   After a considerable pause Mitzi suddenly enters from the kitchen

Mitzi It's all very well saying a knob the size of a nut called filbert, but there's peanuts and coconuts, and ...

Fisher
            } (*together*) OUT!!
Cadwallader

Mitzi Oh, charming.

   Mitzi exits into the kitchen

After another lengthy pause Fisher coughs nervously

Cadwallader Sssh!

Fisher Sorry.

Cadwallader Is my jacket straight?

Fisher Yes, it looks like a straight jacket, sir. (*He looks closer*) Oh, there's a hair on your collar.

Cadwallader Remove it then.

Fisher takes one pace forward and mimes removing it carefully, then sees another and removes it: then another, and another and another including a very long one which is obviously a thread from the suit

(*Exploding*) All right! All right!

Fisher Yes, sir.

There is another pause

Cadwallader Let's hope he speaks English.

Fisher By the way, as he's a Continental would it be rather a nice gesture if I were to kiss him on both cheeks?

Cadwallader You'll stand as far away from him as is humanly possible and keep your mouth shut.

Fisher I meant with my mouth shut.

Cadwallader Kiss him indeed! You are about to meet one of the giant brains of our time. (*He pauses*) Where's the bloody fool got to?

Fisher Could be stuck in the lift. It's always going on the blink.

Cadwallader Trust you to have a lift like that. Come on!

Cadwallader hurries out of the front door

Fisher starts to follow but is sidetracked as ...

Mitzi enters from the kitchen and moves R *towards the balcony, carrying the cookery book*

Fisher Hey! I thought you were supposed to be making the omelette?

Mitzi Yes, it's coming along all right but the recipe says: "At this point leave for two minutes".

Fisher So?

Mitzi So I'm leaving.

Fisher (*grabbing her*) Come here! You leave the omelette, not the room. Get back in there! (*He pushes her back towards the kitchen*)

Cadwallader (*off*) Fisher!! On second thoughts, you take the fire escape.

Fisher Fire escape. Right, sir. (*To Mitzi*) And when it's done shove it in the oven.

Fisher hurriedly exits through the french windows and disappears

Mitzi (*shouting angrily after him*) I know where I'd like to shove it ...

At this moment Lesley Tregunter-Jones enters from the corridor R. *She is a tweedy lady of uncertain age. She carries a large shoulder bag. She is unquestionably British to the core*

Tregunter-Jones Hello, is this the Fisher flat?

Mitzi Yes.

Tregunter-Jones What a relief! (*She enters*) You wouldn't believe the trouble I've had finding the right flat—complete cock-up. I thought the Germans were efficient but they call the first floor the second floor and the ground floor the first floor. (*She sticks out a hand*) You must be Mrs Fisher.

Mitzi winces visibly at Tregunter-Jones's hearty grip and eases her fingers

Mitzi (*hesitant*) Must I?

Tregunter-Jones Miss Tregunter-Jones. Got some very important business to discuss with your husband.

Mitzi He's just stormed out for a minute.

Tregunter-Jones Fine. I'll wait. (*Sitting*) Mind if I take the weight off the old pins? I'm knackered, what with this heat and the amount of free booze

they pour down your gullet when you fly first class. (*She chuckles*) Nearly
went arse over tip coming down the steps.

Mitzi Would you like a drink to cool you down?

Tregunter-Jones Lovely! I'll stick to the same poison—a large g. and t. (*She
rises*) Damn! Got to tinkle. Rather urgent. D'you mind?

Mitzi (*pointing*) I think there's one down the corridor.

Tregunter-Jones (*looking towards the desk*) Don't worry, my dear. I'll do it
here.

Mitzi (*startled*) Pardon?

Tregunter-Jones The phone.

Mitzi (*relieved*) Oh, I see! Help yourself.

Tregunter-Jones Thanks. (*She goes to the desk telephone and dials a long
number*)

Mitzi This business of yours, are you from the sanitary or the vice squad?

Tregunter-Jones (*laughing*) Neither! I'm from Midland Motors to discuss
modifications for our new Cyclone. It's keep-it-under-your-hat time of
course. Some of my colleagues laugh at me but I never even let the
customs see my blueprints. Cautious old Tregunter-Jones tucks anything
confidential in the knickers. (*She pats her thighs, then, to the phone*)
Midland Motors? ... Design Department, please. Extension four....
Ta ...

Mitzi I'll just fetch some ice.

Tregunter-Jones Thanks.

Mitzi (*moving*) If I can find the fridge.

Mitzi exits into the kitchen

Tregunter-Jones (*a double-take*) *Find* the fridge? (*Then, on the telephone*)
Hello? Eric? ... T.J. here. I'm in Berlin. ... Yes, I've done Cologne,
Dusseldorf and Hamburg. ... All according to plan and we've managed
to recall every Cyclone that's been sold this year. ... Well, three actually.
Disaster time for sales. ...

Mitzi returns from the kitchen with a bowl of ice

(*On the phone*) See you Monday. I'm flying back tonight but going
straight down to Romsey to stay with Mumsie. ... Will do. ... 'Bye.

Tregunter-Jones hangs up and turns to Mitzi who is completing the drink

Mitzi Here's your drink.

Tregunter-Jones Thanks. I must say you're a damn sight prettier than the
average Midland Motors spouse. What's your name?

Mitzi Mitzi.

Tregunter-Jones Sweet. I'm Les.

Mitzi Oh, well. It takes all sorts.

Tregunter-Jones is drinking and may be unaware of the misunderstanding

Tregunter-Jones (*drinking deeply*) Whew! Is this gin or gelignite? (*She moves
to the balcony window*) If I'm to discuss faulty gearboxes with due
sobriety, I'd better get a breath of air. (*She moves out*) Super view.

Tregunter-Jones exits on to the balcony

Fisher hurries in through the front door in a bit of a state

Fisher Whoever it was has completely disappeared. You haven't seen anyone looking for me, have you?

Mitzi Yes, on the balcony out there, with something important for you.

Fisher (*joyful*) Hans! You mean he's here?

Mitzi It isn't a "he", it's a "she".

Fisher A woman?!

Mitzi Well, sort of—a bit butch and told me she was les.

Fisher (*to himself*) Of course—master of disguise! A chameleon.

Mitzi Well, she didn't do any good jokes.

Fisher No, not comedian, chameleon.

Mitzi What?

Fisher eagerly moves to a position where he can see Tregunter-Jones on the balcony

Fisher (*looking out to the balcony*) Incredible! It's him!

Mitzi *Him?*

Fisher (*leading her towards the kitchen*) This is not a woman. It's a man.

Mitzi Oh, come on!

Fisher (*deadly serious*) It's true, Mitzi—a man who has just made a terrifying and dangerous journey from behind the Iron Curtain, bringing vital information. Now skedaddle. I have to be alone with her—him—it.

Mitzi No wonder you're scared of the vice squad.

Mitzi exits into the kitchen

Tregunter-Jones enters from the balcony, without the glass

Tregunter-Jones Ah! Peter Fisher! (*Her hand outstretched*)

Fisher (*rushing to her*) You don't have to tell me who *you* are! This is the proudest moment of my life. (*Extending both arms*) Hans!

Tregunter-Jones clearly thinks he means "hands" and duly extends both her hands, too. They clasp one another

Tregunter-Jones Oh, all right.

Fisher Let me look at you. Fantastic! Unbelievable!

Tregunter-Jones (*puzzled*) What is?

Fisher (*carried away*) Absolutely amazing! You—are—a—woman!

Tregunter-Jones (*somewhat bemused*) Well, I try to be.

Fisher And succeed a hundred percent! How do you do it?

Tregunter-Jones How do I do what?

Fisher The whole aura—the voice, the accent and those marvellous clothes. They look straight out of *Country Life*!

Tregunter-Jones Can't think why. Practically slept in them these last few days.

Fisher (*all sympathy*) My God, yes! It must have been pure hell. That journey. But the clothes problem is easily remedied. Take 'em off.

Tregunter-Jones Sorry?

Fisher I'll lend you a suit. You'll feel more at home. Should fit you all right—except for the boobs. They're fantastic!

Tregunter-Jones smiles and moves away from him

Tregunter-Jones Well, thank you very much.

Fisher You must have nerves of steel. What happens if you're stopped and they suddenly decide to give you a strip search? Down to the buff?

Tregunter-Jones Don't worry. I'm fully prepared.

Fisher You can't be. With a woman searching you she'll have a fit when she comes across your thingy.

Tregunter-Jones First hint of a strip search and it's into the loo, whip it out and cut it up.

Fisher (*a shudder*) I beg your pardon?

Tregunter-Jones Then scrumple up the pieces and flush it away.

Fisher You what?

Tregunter-Jones Fortunately I've been lucky. Haven't had to do it once.

Fisher You'd have a hell of a job doing it twice!

Tregunter-Jones Now, are we alone?

Fisher nods

Then, if you like, I'll show it to you now. (*She starts to lift her skirt*)

Fisher No! Please! I'll take your word for it.

Tregunter-Jones No use taking my word. You've got to see it for yourself and the sooner the better.

Fisher But someone might come in.

Tregunter-Jones Don't worry. If anyone comes I can easily scrunch it up and shove it under a cushion.

Fisher Excuse me. I think I may have lost the thread of this conversation.

Tregunter-Jones (*producing a blueprint from under her skirt*) Well, here's the gen. This diagram explains it all.

Fisher (*stopping her unfolding it*) Sorry. Much as I'd like to be the first to see it, I think you'll have to deal direct with Cadwallader.

Tregunter-Jones Cadwallader? Never heard of him. Who's he?

Fisher Cadwallader. You must have heard of him.

Tregunter-Jones Never.

Fisher Never?

Tregunter-Jones No, my orders are to deal direct with you and only you.

Fisher Me?

Tregunter-Jones Yes. You are in charge. Anyone I don't know I don't trust so until I'm very sure he's OK I don't want to meet him. (*She puts the blueprint back in her bag*)

Fisher Right sir . . . ma'am. But just in case you do happen to meet him you should know we call him Maunders.

Tregunter-Jones Maunders?

Fisher He's the butler.

Tregunter-Jones Really?

Fisher No, not really. He's actually Cadwallader who thinks my wife is Moo-Moo the Axe.

Tregunter-Jones (*beginning to reel*) Moo-Moo the Axe?

Fisher (*nodding*) Who chopped up her husband with a meat axe.

Tregunter-Jones Really?

Fisher No, not really, but he thinks she did and that she has just been released from a special home.

Tregunter-Jones Really?

Fisher No. Not really. Really, Monica is the showjumping daughter of an impoverished country vicar.

Tregunter-Jones (*laughing at this*) Not really!

Fisher Yes, really. Oh, and I forgot to mention Heidi the maid who's practically naked, owing to a bad case of prickly heat.

Tregunter-Jones Prickly heat? I suppose there's a reason for all this?

Fisher I think so.

Cadwallader (*yelling, off*) Fisher!

Fisher Now, which one's that? That's Cadwallader!

Tregunter-Jones That's Maunders, right?

Fisher Right. Now you don't want to see him.

Tregunter-Jones No, I'd better disappear. Where do you suggest? (*She picks up her bag*)

Fisher I have a nice semi-detached cupboard over there.

Fisher leads Tregunter-Jones across the room and opens the cupboard door

You'll be all right in there, Hans. You don't mind if I call you Hans?

Tregunter-Jones No, do by all means.

Tregunter-Jones exits into the cupboard

Fisher closes the cupboard door. He walks away, for once thoroughly pleased with himself

Fisher Peter Fisher, you've done it! You're in charge and the big prize is yours! And as for you Mister Cad-rotten-wallader ...

Fisher mimes firing a gun and coincides precisely with the sound of a shot off-stage, followed by a male yell of pain. Fisher is puzzled and shaken

Cadwallader (*off*) Aaah!

Heidi enters DR

Heidi Peter, my darling. I thought Otto had killed you.

Fisher Not me. But somebody's bought it.

Heidi So long as it isn't you, my liebchen.

Fisher No! If Otto suspected me he'd be battering on that door by now.

Someone starts battering loudly on the door

He's battering on the door by now!

In a reflex movement Fisher opens the cupboard door and pushes Heidi inside

Heidi exits into the cupboard

Fisher moves towards the front door while the knocking continues

The cupboard door opens and Tregunter-Jones looks out

Tregunter-Jones "Prickly heat"?
Fisher Well done! (*He gives the thumbs-up signal*)

Tregunter-Jones retires into the cupboard again

Fisher picks up a brolly from the hatstand and stands poised to hit "Otto" over the head. Fisher opens the front door

Come in.

The door opens on to Fisher's face. Cadwallader, bent double and in pain, staggers in

Cadwallader (*hoarsely*) Shut the door. Don't open it to anyone except Hans if he ever shows.

Fisher closes the door. He shouts loudly for Tregunter-Jones's benefit

Fisher (*shouting*) Hullo, Mister *Cadwallader*!
Cadwallader Don't shout!
Fisher You look a bit rough. You all right?
Cadwallader Lucky to be alive. I've been shot.
Fisher Where?
Cadwallader Up the fire escape.
Fisher Nasty. How far up?
Cadwallader Near the top.
Fisher It wasn't a big fellow who accused you of seducing his wife?
Cadwallader When did I have the time to seduce anybody?
Fisher I don't know how long you take.
Cadwallader No, it was one of my own men. Bloody fool tripped over his gun, let fly, and got me in the backside.
Fisher Pretty painful eh! Let me fetch the doctor.
Cadwallader No! He might send me to hospital and I can't leave here until Hans has reported in.
Fisher How many pellets did you stop?
Cadwallader How the hell should I know?
Fisher You told me you had eyes in the back of your head.
Cadwallader Shut up and take a look.

Cadwallader bends over. Fisher raises the flaps of his jacket, looks and whistles

Fisher Whew! One hundred and eighty!

Monica, now dressed, enters UL. *She approaches unseen, rivetted by what goes on*

A bull's-eye and two double tops! (*He sees Monica behind him*) I'm afraid Maunders has had a little accident.
Monica It doesn't look like a little accident to me. It looks as if he's been shot.
Fisher Right on target, Moo-Moo. He was accidentally shot up the fire escape.

Monica Then we must call the doctor.

Cadwallader (*seizing the phone*) No! I refuse.

Monica I'm not risking you getting septicaemia while you're in my care, but fortunately *I* can attend to you. I am a trained nurse.

Cadwallader My God! It's "doctors and nurses" day!

Monica Don't panic. I have a very steady hand.

Cadwallader Please! Not the chopper!

Monica (*laughing*) We'll only use the chopper as a last resort!

Cadwallader shudders

> *Monica exits* UL

Cadwallader I'm trapped—trapped.

Cadwallader, now in a complete panic, whips out one red and one white handkerchief and starts desperately semaphoring a message, standing near the cupboard. From the opposite side of the room Fisher watches this in stunned fascination for some moments

Fisher The pellets have reached his brain.

Cadwallader continues desperately to semaphore. Fisher now takes out his two birthday handkerchiefs and in reply does a Morris dance proceeding towards Cadwallader

> *Cadwallader finally gives up and, before Fisher can stop him, dives into the cupboard and slams the door shut behind him*

No! (*He looks at his watch and counts again*) One—two—three——

Cadwallader comes out, and closes door again

Cadwallader What the hell's going on?

Fisher (*wearily*) Now what's the matter?

Cadwallader There are two people in that cupboard.

Fisher Of course.

Cadwallader You mean you know?

Fisher Of course.

Cadwallader One of them is the maid, half-naked.

Fisher Of course.

Cadwallader The other is a stranger, a woman, and don't say "of course".

Fisher Of course not.

Cadwallader Who is she?

Fisher You know who that is.

Cadwallader I don't.

Fisher You must do. Just arrived.

Cadwallader I tell you I don't ... (*He stiffens and his voice drops to a whisper*) It isn't?

Fisher It is!

Cadwallader Hans!

Fisher No, the doctor.

Cadwallader Doctor?

Fisher From the hospital.
Cadwallader Which hospital?
Fisher The hosp . . . the sanatorium. She's come to take back Moo-Moo the
  Axe.
Cadwallader Ah! That's the best news I've had all day. (*Then he frowns*)
  Wait a minute. I thought they'd only just let her out?
Fisher Yes, but now they're taking her back.
Cadwallader Why?
Fisher Well, they've just made a rather nasty discovery at the sanatorium.
Cadwallader What and where?
Fisher Her old doctor. (*A slight thought*) In a drawer.
Cadwallader A drawer!
Fisher Well, two or three drawers actually. His legs wouldn't fit so she went
  one, two, three. (*He makes three chopping movements*) Three drawers.
Cadwallader Shut up! Shut up! I've just had an idea. Let's get that doctor in
  here. She can attend to my injury before I meet Hans.
Fisher Hans? I don't think that's quite up her street.
Cadwallader Nonsense. A doctor's a doctor.

*Cadwallader strides to the cupboard before Fisher can stop him and opens the
door*

  Madam, would you step in here a moment?

Tregunter-Jones comes out warily with her bag

Tregunter-Jones Yes?
Cadwallader I——
Fisher (*cutting in*) Nice of you to pop out *doctor*. We won't keep you a
  minute, *doctor*; just a slight medicinal problem has arisen, doctor, and we
  feel you may be able to deal with it seeing that you're a doctor, *doctor*.
Cadwallader All right! All right! We all know she's a doctor!
Fisher (*to Tregunter-Jones*) Do we?
Tregunter-Jones Ah—yes. (*To Cadwallader*) I'm a doctor.
Cadwallader I know! Before I raise my own little problem, doctor, I would
  like to express my deepest sympathy about that dreadful discovery.
Tregunter-Jones Where?
Cadwallader In your drawers.
Tregunter-Jones I beg your pardon?
Cadwallader Well. I assumed they were your drawers since it was——
Fisher (*cutting in*) She'd rather not talk about it. (*Sotto*) Still very cut up.
Tregunter-Jones What exactly is this gentleman's problem?
Fisher Well, funnily enough, it's in *his* drawers!
Cadwallader No laughing matter. I've got half a dozen shotgun pellets in
  my backside and I'd be greatly obliged if you would dig them out.

*Tregunter-Jones sways slightly and rocks on her heels but keeps admirable
control*

Tregunter-Jones Very sorry. No can do. (*She puts her bag on the sofa*)
Cadwallader Why not?

Tregunter-Jones (*at a loss*) Ahm ...

Fisher Because she's a cosmetic surgeon.

Cadwallader But that's ideal ...

Fisher No. She only does faces not backsides. (*To Tregunter-Jones*) Am I right, doctor?

Tregunter-Jones Absolutely.

Fisher Though some of her faces looked like backsides, but that's another story.

Cadwallader (*late reaction*) Cosmetic surgery? Are you asking me to believe you do nose jobs and facelifts ... for the criminally insane?

Tregunter-Jones (*lost again*) Well ...

Fisher (*leaping to the rescue*) Yes. You're looking at a saint, Mr Maunders. The doctor here has devoted her life to the poor unfortunate inmates in the—er—thingy.

Cadwallader Oh, hospice!

Fisher (*hurt*) All right, don't believe me, but please remember there is a lady present.

Cadwallader (*angrily*) There are far too many ladies present. (*Producing his gun*) You've got one minute to get rid of them.

Fisher Could I have two?

Cadwallader No. Remember Tubby Fanshaw.

Fisher (*going to Tregunter-Jones*) Doctor, could you come back next week?

Heidi comes out from the cupboard

Heidi I am so fed up with all this dusting and cleaning.

Fisher Yes, I know, but you must go back in there.

Heidi But it's so hot.

Fisher (*rushing up*) Well, take something off. (*He pushes her back in*)

Heidi exits into the cupboard

Mitzi rushes in with an omelette on a plate

Mitzi I've done it. I've made an omelette!

Fisher We don't want it now.

Mitzi (*furious*) You what? I could kill you!

Fisher So could he, so just get in there. (*He pushes Mitzi into the cupboard*)

Mitzi exits into the cupboard

Fisher slams the door

Monica enters with a tray of water and antiseptic, etc.

Monica I'm all ready for you now, Maunders.

Cadwallader (*backing away with his hand on his gun*) Keep her away from me.

Fisher Right. This way please. (*He starts to push her towards the cupboard*)

Monica Have you gone mad?

Fisher Yes.

Monica (*seeing Tregunter-Jones*) Who's this?

Tregunter-Jones I'm the doctor.

Fisher She's come about Maunders' little problem.

Monica You sent for her?

Fisher No. She just happened to be passing, heard a shot and popped in on the offchance.

Mitzi comes out of the cupboard with an empty plate. She shuts the door and gives everyone a little smile

Mitzi She's eaten it!

Fisher Oh good.

Mitzi exits to the kitchen

Monica Who's eaten it?

Fisher One of the doctor's patients.

Monica In a cupboard?

Fisher Well, where else would you treat a patient with advanced prickly heat who must be kept in the dark and fed on a light diet of omelettes?

Monica How silly of me to ask. Excuse me, I won't keep you long, Maunders.

She exits to the kitchen

Tregunter-Jones Who is that lady?

Fisher Moo-Moo the Axe.

Cadwallader Whom you should be taking back to the sanatorium.

Tregunter-Jones Oh yes. I didn't recognize her without my glasses.

Fisher She's as blind as a bat.

Cadwallader Don't start that again. Get her out of here.

Monica pops her head in

Monica Could you spare a moment, doctor?

Tregunter-Jones Certainly. Excuse me.

Tregunter-Jones exits to the kitchen

Cadwallader goes to the drinks table and pours three brandies

Cadwallader If you can't get rid of these women I can. Fortunately I have a little something here which will effectively eliminate them. (*He takes a phial from his pocket and puts a drop from it into each brandy glass*)

Fisher Now look! I will not be a party to murder.

Cadwallader Not murder, you twit. It's a knock-out drop, paralyses instantly from the neck down.

Fisher For how long?

Cadwallader (*chuckling*) Permanently, unless someone knows the trick to get you out of it. (*He puts down the drinks on the table by the sofa. To make room he picks up Tregunter-Jones's shoulder bag to move it and sees the blueprint. He picks it up and examines it*)

Fisher I don't like the idea of this drugging——

Cadwallader (*cutting in*) What's this! What genuine doctor would carry a blueprint like this!

Fisher also examines the blueprint and looks genuinely puzzled

Fisher That's funny. It looks like the gearbox on the new Cyclone.

Cadwallader (*hugely excited*) Yes! Can't you see what this means?

Fisher No.

Cadwallader (*pointing to the kitchen*) That *isn't* a doctor. It's Hans! Yes, Hans, disguised as a woman rep from Midland Motors. (*He waves the blueprint*) And this is our million pound jackpot!

Fisher (*more and more puzzled*) But it says it's the modified gearbox of the Cyclone.

Cadwallader Of course it does, you dumb cluck! It's meant to look like that in case Hans is stopped and searched on his way here. But soak this in water and the formula of the miracle battery will appear like magic.

Fisher (*believing this*) I see.

Cadwallader Brilliant! Didn't I tell you what a genius he is at disguise?

Fisher (*chuckling*) Yes, that's what I said to him when we met. I said: "Hans, you are fantas——" (*He realizes his slip*) I mean I *nearly* said: "Hans" ... I mean, I would have said: "Hans" if I ...

Cadwallader suddenly grasps him with the crook of his arm in a lethal grip round the throat

Cadwallader You knew! You knew all along this was Hans.

Fisher (*strangled*) Well, I ...

Cadwallader *You* invented that doctor story to fool me.

Fisher Yes, but only ...

Cadwallader You tried to double-cross me.

Fisher No. It was Hans. He insisted his orders were to deal with nobody but me.

Cadwallader Hand over the world's most valuable document to *you*?

Fisher makes an ineffectual grab at it

Fisher Yes.

Cadwallader (*jerking it away*) Oh, no you don't, you little snake-in-the-grass! This is my pigeon. There's a knighthood waiting for the person who gets this—and it's going to be me.

Monica enters from the kitchen

Monica Wrong. It's going to be me. Hands up!

Cadwallader turns and leaps back as Monica produces a gun and points it in their direction

Cadwallader My God! She's going to shoot us! Fisher, you said she only used the axe.

Fisher Moo-Moo, what are you doing with that gun?

Monica Nothing at the moment, dear, but don't tempt me. (*To Cadwallader*) I'll have Hans's formula please.

Monica takes the blueprint from Cadwallader

Cadwallader (*staggered*) Hans? You know about Hans?

Monica You don't really think I fell for that idiotic doctor story, do you? That had to be Hans. (*She waves the blueprint*) And this is what we are all looking for.

Cadwallader All! (*Enraged*) Fisher, you've been harbouring a bloody commy agent!

Fisher Moo-Moo! Say it isn't true. Say you're just a simple idiot like me.

Monica has moved to the desk and presses a button on the intercom

Monica (*laughing*) No-one could be an idiot like you, Peterkins. Kurt?

Kurt's Voice (*off*) Bitte? Hier ist Kurt.

Monica Operation Hans complete. Opposition immobilized and objective safely in our hands.

Kurt's Voice (*off; American accent*) Great! Then I can drop this goddam German accent. I'll be waiting, honey.

Monica (*making a kissing sound*) Like you always are, my angel.

Kurt's Voice And Washington here we come!

Cadwallader A *Yankee* spy! They're the worst!

Monica No, the best. The CIA are paying us two million for this.

Fisher (*desolated*) Moo-Moo!

Heidi enters UL. She stops, astonished, at seeing Monica with a gun

Heidi Wass ist das?

Monica Das ist ein gun, dear. Now back into your favourite hidey-hole and carry on spring cleaning. (*Another laugh*) And someone will spring you, eventually.

Heidi exits into the cupboard, shepherded by Monica

As Monica locks the cupboard door, Cadwallader makes a surreptitious movement designed to start a counter-attack. He gestures to Fisher to help

(*Without turning*) Don't try it boys. I've eyes in the back of my head.

Fisher Not another one!

Monica now turns and gestures with the gun

Monica Move! Stand side by side in front of the sofa.

Cadwallader and Fisher obviously feel their end is near and both panic as they move to the sofa

Cadwallader ⎱ (*together*) Help! Mitzi! Hans! Help!
Fisher ⎰

Monica It's no use calling Hans or Mitzi. They're both very "tied up" I'm afraid. I think this calls for a toast, don't you?

Cadwallader (*a ray of hope*) Yes! Help yourself. On the table here.

Monica Pick up those glasses.

This causes further panic

Cadwallader Not for me. I'm a teetotaller.
Fisher Never touch it.
Cadwallader But don't let us stop you.

Monica raises the gun menacingly

Monica I give you three seconds. One . . . two . . .

Cadwallader and Fisher both grab the glasses

Cadwallader Your very good health.
Fisher Astonishing luck.

Cadwallader and Fisher both drink

I thought you said it was instant . . .

Now Cadwallader and Fisher react as if they have been hit over the head. They jump, stagger, choke, grasp their throats then collapse side by side on the sofa. They are conscious but paralysed. Fisher tilts sideways and rests his head on Cadwallader's shoulder

Monica I should have warned you that as well as eyes in the back of my head, I also have a very good pair of ears. Good-bye my battered old "Escort". (*She moves across to the front door and opens it*)
Fisher Moo-Moo, when did you start deceiving me?
Monica Remember Kitzbuhel?
Fisher That was our honeymoon!
Monica Yes, well, just before that.

Monica exits through the front door

Fisher Never trust a vicar's daughter.
Cadwallader God, it's frustrating! You see, I know how to get out of this. All we need is two fingers pressed on the back of the neck.

The kitchen door opens and Mitzi and Tregunter-Jones come out. Both women look the worse for wear and both are removing pieces of cord which have been binding their arms

Cadwallader ⎫
Fisher ⎭ (*together*) Thank Heaven! Hans! Mitzi! Saved.
Mitzi Don't you Mitzi me! Bound and gagged by that nutty woman. Lucky I do an act with ropes.
Fisher Quick! It may not be too late . . .
Tregunter-Jones (*thunderous*) It's too late for you, Fisher. You are sacked from Midland Motors as of now.
Fisher (*stunned*) Midland Mo——? What are you . . .?
Tregunter-Jones (*carrying on*) You're a disgrace to the British Motor Trade. Look at you, lolling there drunk; nasty little pervert. (*She picks up her shoulder bag, pats it but does not look inside it. Tapping her bag*) I am not handing over my blueprint to you. I am taking it back to Birmingham. You'd better start packing.

Fisher now realizes the truth and almost loses his voice

Fisher Oh, my God! You're a rep from Midland Motors! You *are* a woman.
Tregunter-Jones What did you think I was—a man?
Fisher Yes. We need help . . .
Mitzi You're damn right you do. Psychiatric mostly, but you ain't getting it
from me. You're all bleeding filberts. (*She grabs her helmet and gear from
the hatstand*)
Cadwallader Help! All we need is two fingers . . .
Tregunter-Jones Shall we, my dear?
Mitzi Why not?

> *Mitzi and Tregunter-Jones then both give an emphatic two-finger salute in
> unison before they exit through the front door*

Fisher And still no Hans.

Cadwallader gives an audible chuckle

> You can laugh but I've lost my wife and my job.
Cadwallader Correction. You've lost your wife and *both* your jobs. And I
can afford to laugh. Poor old Moo-Moo the Axe has sloped off to the CIA
with a load of rubbish!
Fisher So she has! They won't pay her two million for some car modifications.
Cadwallader *She'll* get the chop this time!

> *The cupboard door bursts dramatically open and Heidi jumps out with a
> karate shout*

Heidi Hiyaaaa!
Cadwallader By jingo! I'd forgotten "Prickly Heat"!
Fisher Heidi, help!
Heidi (*running to Fisher*) Peter darling! What can I do?
Cadwallader I'll tell you what to do. I want you to press two fingers behind
my right ear!

She presses

> Press hard with the thumb and forefinger. Twice.

*Heidi does as she is told and Cadwallader is instantly freed. He stands up,
stretching his limbs. Fisher, who has been leaning on him, collapses prone on
the couch. Heidi moves to help him but Cadwallader pushes her aside*

> All right. I'll cope and I'd like a word with him alone.
Heidi (*to Fisher*) I will come back, my darling.

> *Heidi exits UR*

Fisher, meanwhile, has toppled the other way

Fisher Help me.
Cadwallader (*imitating Heidi*) "I will come back, my darling". You never
stop, do you?

Cadwallader heaves him up and presses the back of his neck. Fisher recovers the use of his limbs and stands up groggily

Fisher Thanks. That's better. No more silly mistakes, eh? (*He picks up his glass*) Cheers!

Before Cadwallader can stop him, Fisher drains the glass and is instantly paralysed again. He lies on the sofa with his legs in the air

Cadwallader You nitwit! (*He releases Fisher again*) Hopeless!
Fisher Sorry. Not feeling myself.

An oblong parcel wrapped in brown paper drops through the letter box of the front door

What's that?

Cadwallader, who is nearest to the door, picks it up

Cadwallader Parcel for you from someone called Hans . . .

It suddenly hits them both

Fisher   ⎱
Cadwallader ⎰ (*together*) HANS!

Fisher tears off the envelope attached to the parcel which contains a card

Cadwallader What's it say?
Fisher (*reading*) "Sorry, cannot come in person; but hope the film proves instructive. Regards. Hans."
Cadwallader This is it! He's delivered it on film! (*He seizes it from Fisher*) And here's my knighthood. It's mine.
Fisher I beg your pardon. It's addressed to me. It's mine.
Cadwallader No, it's mine.
Fisher No it's not. It's mine.

Fisher stamps his foot angrily and inadvertently treads on Cadwallader's foot. Cadwallader yells, hops away and sits heavily on the chair in front of the desk. This causes him acute pain in his rear. He now nurses both rear and feet

Cadwallader Oooh!
Heidi (*off*) Peter darling!
Cadwallader It's Heidi! Hide it!

Fisher stuffs the packet down the front of his trousers, concealing it, as . . .

Heidi enters now wearing a dress of Monica's and carrying a shoulder bag

Heidi I will have to leave. Our two hours is up. (*She puts her arms round his neck*) Good-bye, my darling. (*She presses herself against him*) Oh, Peter . . . (*Then she reacts to the hard lump made by the packet*) Oh, *Peter*! (*She looks down*) What have we got down there?
Fisher Nothing.
Heidi I think it is something for me.
Fisher No, it's private. And it's mine.

Heidi (*struggling with him*) No, darling, it's mine. (*She pulls out the packet and runs to the front door, laughing*)
Fisher Don't mess about. Give that back.
Heidi No, darling, this is the formula I have been waiting for.
Fisher
Cadwallader } (*together*) What!

Cadwallader leaps to his feet. Heidi whips out a gun from her shoulder bag

Heidi Stay where you are, both of you.
Fisher (*stricken*) Heidi! You too?
Heidi Yes, I'm sorry it was not a real love affair. And don't try to follow me. Otto is outside with orders to kill anyone who comes out of here.
Cadwallader God, your maid's a German spy!
Heidi No, Mister Cadwallader. I work for a Japanese consortium. Sayonara!

Heidi exits, closing the door

Fisher Ah so!
Cadwallader And the same to you.
Fisher I bet she's bluffing. I won't let her get away with this.

Fisher opens the front door. There is an instant gunshot and woodwork splinters. Fisher hastily comes back, closing the door, and drawer 1 opens fast. Fisher closes drawer 1 and turns round. Drawer 2 opens and pushes Fisher on the bottom. He closes drawer 2. There is more gunfire and he drops to his knees. Drawer 1 opens fast and Fisher bangs his head as he gets up

Cadwallader (*chuckling*) Hah! You nearly had a nasty accident there.
Fisher I think I'm having it now.
Cadwallader So she wasn't bluffing. That means total failure. That's it. I'm off.
Fisher Back to the UK?
Cadwallader No, to Moscow.
Fisher *You*? Going to Moscow?
Cadwallader I daren't show my face in London after this and I've had some interesting approaches from the Commies over the years.
Fisher But could you desert your family, your friends?
Cadwallader I've dozens of friends over there.
Fisher Russians?
Cadwallader No! A lot of old chums from M.I.5 and Cambridge.

A sound of muffled shouting is heard offstage. This attracts Fisher's attention. He opens the front door an inch and carefully peeks out. Then closes the door

Fisher There's a hell of a row going on. I say! I think Heidi's stuck in the lift!

Cadwallader turns and runs to his briefcase

Cadwallader Then there's still a chance to beat them to the ground floor, over the balcony.

Fisher You can't jump into the canal! We're four floors up. You'll kill yourself.

Cadwallader takes out a length of rope from his briefcase. NB. This is elasticized rope

Cadwallader I'm not going to, you fool. I came prepared. Hang on to the rope, pay it out gently and for God's sake don't let go or I'm a dead duck.
Fisher Oh, right.

Fisher takes one end. Cadwallader wraps the other end round himself like a climber. He climbs up on to the wall of balcony

Cadwallader *Au revoir.*

Cadwallader jumps

Fisher is immediately pulled fast forward

Fisher *Auf Wieders-e-h-e-e-en!*

Fisher regains control just in time and fights his way back. He is standing by the sofa when he comes across Hans's note again and picks it up

Hey! Are you still there?
Cadwallader *(off)* Where the hell do you think I am?
Fisher That parcel. It's from my Hans, not your Hans. It's a birthday present from my friend Hans Gruber of Volkswagen.
Cadwallader *(off)* What?
Fisher It's a porno video film. The real Hans hasn't turned up yet so Heidi's gone off to Japan with a blue movie!
Cadwallader *(off)* Then stop gassing and pull me up.
Fisher Right, sir.

Fisher starts to pull Cadwallader back and knocks his hand against the radio, thus turning it on. It starts to play "The Ride Of the Valkyries". He then has a tremendous struggle being dragged towards the balcony, then gaining ground again, climbing back over the sofa. (NB. At all times, wherever Fisher is, the rope must be kept at full tension)

During this a helicopter is heard approaching. The noise of its engine grows louder. A red light flashes and papers can be blown around as if blown by the rotors. A man's legs appear outside the window as he is lowered by a rope from the helicopter. Between his feet the man clutches a metal box with a big red star on it. (NB. If this is not possible then the box can be hooked on to the end of a rope)

(Yelling) Hans?
Foot's Voice *(off)* No. FEET!

Still clinging to the rope Fisher struggles and grabs the box from the man's feet. As soon as he has done this the man disappears upwards again and the noise of the helicopter swiftly recedes. Fisher, clinging to both rope and box, comes back into the middle of the room

Fisher We've won! Hans has delivered!
Cadwallader (*off*) Great! Pull me up!
Fisher Right, sir.

Fisher starts foot by foot to haul Cadwallader up. All goes smoothly until the phone rings

Oh, damn! (*He shouts*) Hang on!

Fisher automatically lets go of the rope to pick up the phone. The rope whips across the room and out over the balcony like lightning and Cadwallader presumably falls to his doom. Fisher drops the receiver and stretches out a futile hand towards the balcony as——

the CURTAIN *falls*

However, there is a postscript and the action of the play is continued as follows:

During the curtain call Cadwallader limps in covered in mud and river weed

FURNITURE AND PROPERTY LIST

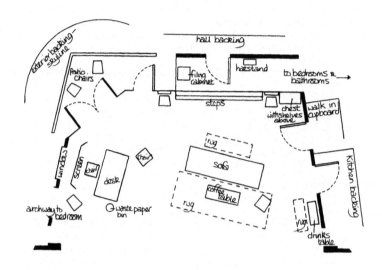

ACT I

On stage: Sofa. *On it:* cushions, rug

Coffee table. *On it:* cigarette box with cigarettes, lighter, ashtray, car and fishing magazines

Drinks table. *On it:* bottles of whisky, gin, brandy, tonic water, soda syphon with soda, ice bucket with ice, water jug, dish of lemon slices, glasses

Chest. *On it:* vase of flowers. *On shelves above:* books, radio

By front door: **Monica's** suitcase (heavy) and vanity case

Hatstand. *On it:* various coats, hats, umbrella, pair of boots on floor

Filing cabinet. *On top:* filing tray with books and brochures. *In top drawer:* files. *In drawer 2:* codebook (*NB. Top drawer open—see Filing Cabinet effects plot*)

Several chairs

Desk. *On it:* telephone, intercom, notebook, filing tray with brochures, diary, papers concealing code letter, pens, blotter, paper knife, model cars, "Peter Fisher" nameplate, 2 birthday cards on display. *In drawers:* car brochures, bottle of whisky, glass, scissors for **Monica** in Act II

Swivel chairs either side of desk. *On upstage one:* **Fisher's** jacket over back

Waste-paper basket
Screen
On walls: car posters including one for *Midland Motors New Cyclone*,
   Matterhorn poster
In walk-in cupboard: buckets, brooms, etc., key in door
Carpet and rugs on floor, also various piles of box files, posters, brochures
Window curtains (open)
On kitchen door: detachable door handle and spindle (for **Fisher** to pull off
   on page 24)
On balcony: 2 patio chairs, scattered leaves

Off stage: Pile of letters **(Fisher)**
Wrapped present of 2 handkerchiefs, handbag **(Heidi)**
Shopping basket containing salami, posy of flowers with card, handbag
   (Monica)
Briefcase containing elasticized rope and binoculars, umbrella **(Cadwal-
   lader)**
Handbag **(Heidi)**
Piece of paper **(Mitzi)**
Frying pan **(Mitzi)**
Handbag **(Monica)**
Feather duster, pinafore **(Heidi)**
Egg, straw **(Mitzi)**
Jar of cold cream **(Monica)**

Personal: **Fisher:** keys, wrist-watch
Heidi: florists' card in top of dress
Monica: wrist-watch
Cadwallader: gun in shoulder holster, bleeper in pocket, wrist-watch
Mitzi: wrist-watch

ACT II

Check: **Mitzi**'s helmet etc. on hatstand
Cadwallader's briefcase containing binoculars and elasticized rope
Scissors in desk drawer
Key in walk-in cupboard door

Off stage: Smoking frying pan **(Mitzi)**
Binoculars **(Cadwallader)**
Cookery book **(Mitzi)**—required twice
Shoulder bag **(Tregunter-Jones)**
Bowl of ice **(Mitzi)**
A dress of Monica's **(Heidi)**
Omelette on plate **(Mitzi)**
Tray with bowl of water, antiseptic, cotton-wool, etc. **(Monica)**
Empty plate **(Mitzi)**
Gun **(Monica)**
Cords round arms **(Tregunter-Jones** and **Mitzi)**
Parcel with card in envelope attached **(Stage Management)**
Bag containing gun **(Heidi)**
Metal box with red star on it **(Foot** or **Stage Management)**
Mud and river weed for curtain call **(Cadwallader)**

Personal: **Fisher:** wrist-watch, keys, 2 birthday handkerchiefs in pocket
Cadwallader: wrist-watch, gun in shoulder holster, bleeper, 2 handker-
chiefs, one red, one white, phial of liquid
Monica: wrist-watch
Mitzi: wrist-watch
Tregunter-Jones: wrist-watch, blueprint

LIGHTING PLOT

Property fittings required: *nil*
Interior. An office/living-room. The same scene throughout

ACT I   Morning

To open: Bright interior lighting, hot sunny exterior lighting

No cues

ACT II   Morning

To open: As ACT I

Cue 1   Sound of helicopter approaching and hovering above   (Page 53)
         Flashing red light off above balcony

EFFECTS PLOT

ACT 1

Cue 1   **As CURTAIN rises**   (Page 1)
Music from radio: "The Ride of the Valkyries"; traffic noise off in background

Cue 2   **Fisher** turns off radio   (Page 1)
Cut music; gradually fade traffic noise

Cue 3   **Fisher:** "'Dear Fisher, Operation imminent ...'"   (Page 2)
Doorbell

Cue 4   **Monica:** "... into the kitchen."   (Page 6)
Telephone

Cue 5   **Fisher** walks away from filing cabinet to sofa   (Page 7)
Doorbell

Cue 6   **Fisher:** "... never have let him out."   (Page 8)
Doorbell

Cue 7   **Fisher:** "Oh, forget it!" (*He flips "Off" switch*)   (Page 13)
Doorbell and telephone

Cue 8   **Mitzi** walks into walk-in cupboard   (Page 16)
Crashes, off

Cue 9   **Fisher:** "Just stretching my legs."   (Page 18)
Telephone

Cue 10   **Cadwallader:** "They're ruthless."   (Page 22)
High-pitched bleeper sounds

Cue 11   **Cadwallader:** "Acknowledge."   (Page 22)
High-pitched gabble from bleeper—cut after a short while

Cue 12   **Cadwallader** exits through french windows on to balcony   (Page 22)
Doorbell

Cue 13   **Fisher** moves L towards the drinks   (Page 25)
Thump from walk-in cupboard

ACT II

Cue 14   **Cadwallader:** "... as crazy as the rest of you."   (Page 32)
High-pitched bleeper sounds

Cue 15   **Cadwallader:** "Acknowledge."   (Page 32)
Gabble from bleeper—cut after a few seconds

Cue 16   **Cadwallader:** "... I mean, yes madam." (*He curtsies*)   (Page 34)
Crash from kitchen

Cue 17	**Monica** opens kitchen door, pops her head inside *Another crash*	(Page 34)
Cue 18	**Cadwallader:** "How does she manage to ...?" *High-pitched bleeper sounds*	(Page 35)
Cue 19	**Cadwallader:** "Acknowledge." *Short, unintelligible message from bleeper*	(Page 36)
Cue 20	**Fisher** mimes firing a gun *Gunshot, off*	(Page 41)
Cue 21	**Fisher:** "... get away with this." (*He opens the front door*) *Gunshot and splintering wood*	(Page 52)
Cue 22	**Fisher** closes drawer 2 in filing cabinet *Gunfire*	(Page 52)
Cue 23	**Fisher** knocks his hand against radio, turning it on *Music from radio: "The Ride of the Valkyries"*	(Page 53)
Cue 24	As **Fisher** struggles, pulling on rope *Helicopter approaches—increase engine noise until helicopter is supposedly above balcony—papers blown around in room; fade radio as helicopter arrives*	(Page 53)
Cue 25	**Fisher** grabs box from **Foot** *Fade out helicopter as it flies off*	(Page 53)
Cue 26	**Fisher** starts foot by foot to haul **Cadwallader** up *Telephone*	(Page 54)

FILING CABINET EFFECTS PLOT

Instructions for working filing cabinet by Stage Management off-stage

ACT I

To open: Drawer 1 (top) open

Cue 1	**Fisher** puts papers and letters into drawer 1 and closes it *Drawer 2 opens slowly to ¾*	(Page 1)
Cue 2	**Fisher:** "'Dear Fisher, Operation imminent.'" Doorbell rings. **Fisher** begins to close drawer 2 *Stop drawer 2 closing, open drawer 1—both drawers are open together*	(Page 2)
Cue 3	**Fisher** tries to close both drawers *Momentarily hold both drawers open, then let go*	(Page 2)
Cue 4	**Fisher** (*to himself*) "... With a mallet." He opens drawer 2, takes out codebook and papers and closes it *Drawer 1 opens slowly*	(Page 7)
Cue 5	Front doorbell rings; **Fisher** closes drawer 1 *Drawer 2 opens slowly*	(Page 7)
Cue 6	**Fisher** closes drawer 2 *Drawer 1 opens fast and hits him on the head*	(Page 7)
Cue 7	**Fisher** closes drawer 1 *Simultaneously drawer 4 opens fast and gets him on the shin*	(Page 7)

ACT II

To open: all drawers shut

Cue 8	Gunshot off; **Fisher** comes back, closing door *Drawer 1 opens fast*	(Page 52)
Cue 9	**Fisher** closes drawer 1 *Drawer 2 opens and pushes him on the bottom*	(Page 52)
Cue 10	**Fisher** closes drawer 2 *Drawer 1 opens fast and **Fisher** bangs his head*	(Page 52)

Lightning Source UK Ltd.
Milton Keynes UK
UKOW06f0208101217

314198UK00003B/8/P

9 780573 016066